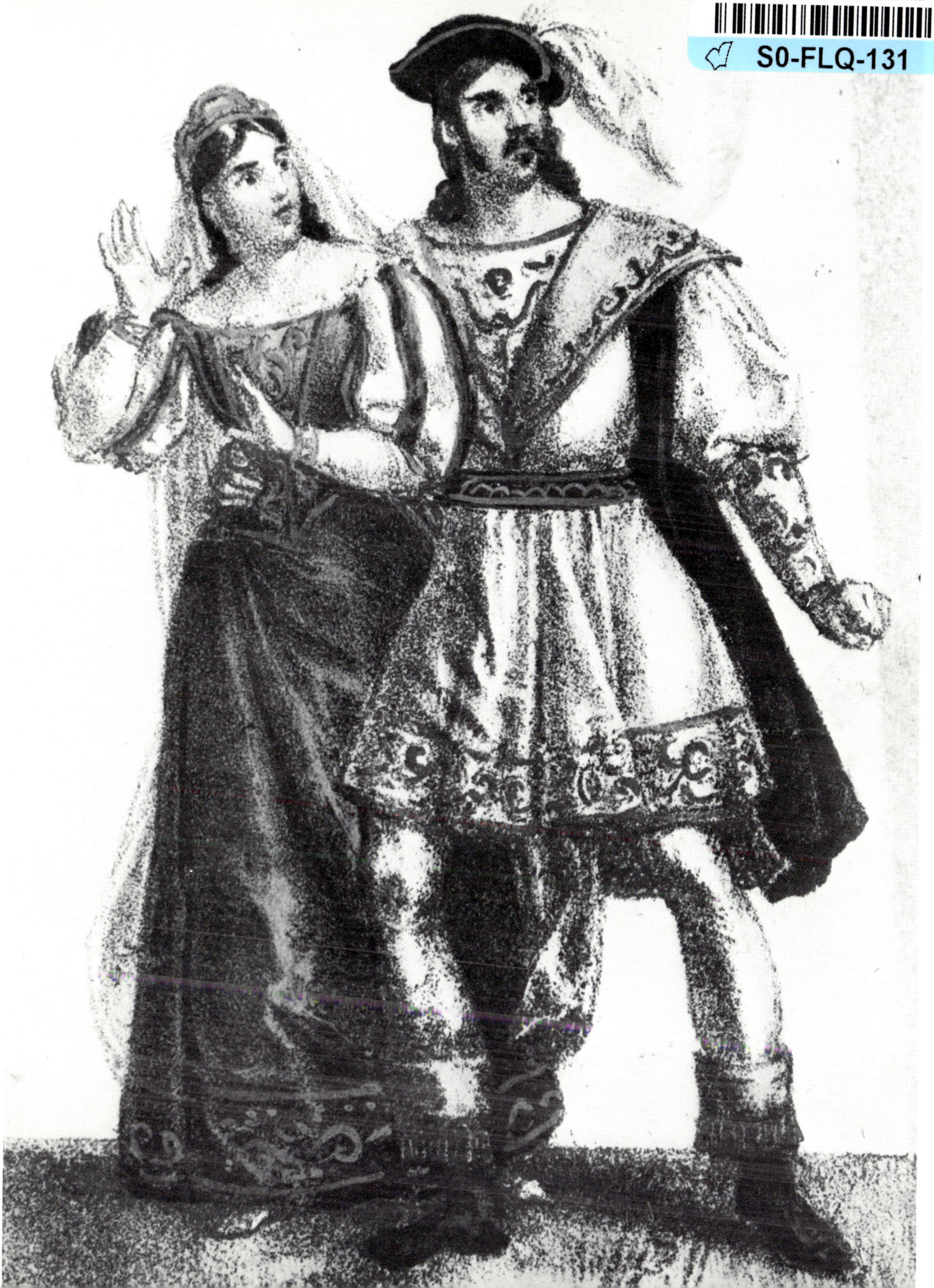

S0-FLQ-131

SIXTY YEARS
1815-1875
by edwin binney 3rd

ITALIAN DANCE PRINTS

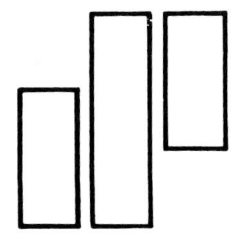

DANCE PERSPECTIVES 53   SPRING, 1973

SELMA JEANNE COHEN, editor
CLELL MIZE, art director
JOHN MARTIN, consulting editor

Edwin Denby, Ivor Guest, Shirley Wimmer, advisory board

Published quarterly by Dance Perspectives Foundation, 29 East 9th Street, New York, N.Y. 10003. Subscription rates: U.S. and Canada: 1 year, $8.00; 2 years, $15.50; 3 years, $23.00. Foreign rates: 50¢ additional each year. Single copies: $2.95.
Second class postage paid at New York, N.Y.

Copyright © 1973 by Dance Perspectives Foundation. All rights reserved. No part of this book may be reproduced in any form or by any electronic or mechanical means including information storage and retrieval systems without permission in writing from the publisher, except by a reviewer who may quote brief passages in a review.

Library of Congress Catalog Card Number: 73-76644

PICTURE CREDITS. The Author: pp. 10, 12, and nos. 50, 55, 84 var A, 86, 105, 109, 184, 189, 196, 222, 229, 234, 237, 275, 387, 417, 436, 460, 464. Photos by Ian Riddell. Zachary C. Solov: no. 144. Harvard Theatre Collection: nos. 10, 21, 33, 69, 102, 112, 183, 231. Photos by Ian Riddell. Dance Collection, The New York Public Library: nos. 22, 37, 83, 119, 122, 134, 156, 177, 187, 206, 239, 257, 443. Photos by Roy Blakey. Raccolta delle Stampe e dei Disegni Castello Sforzesco, Milan: pp. 7, 11, and nos. 16 var, 42, 167, 256. Theatrical Museum, La Scala: nos. 51, 142, 239, 405, 433.

No. 16. Fanny Cerrito

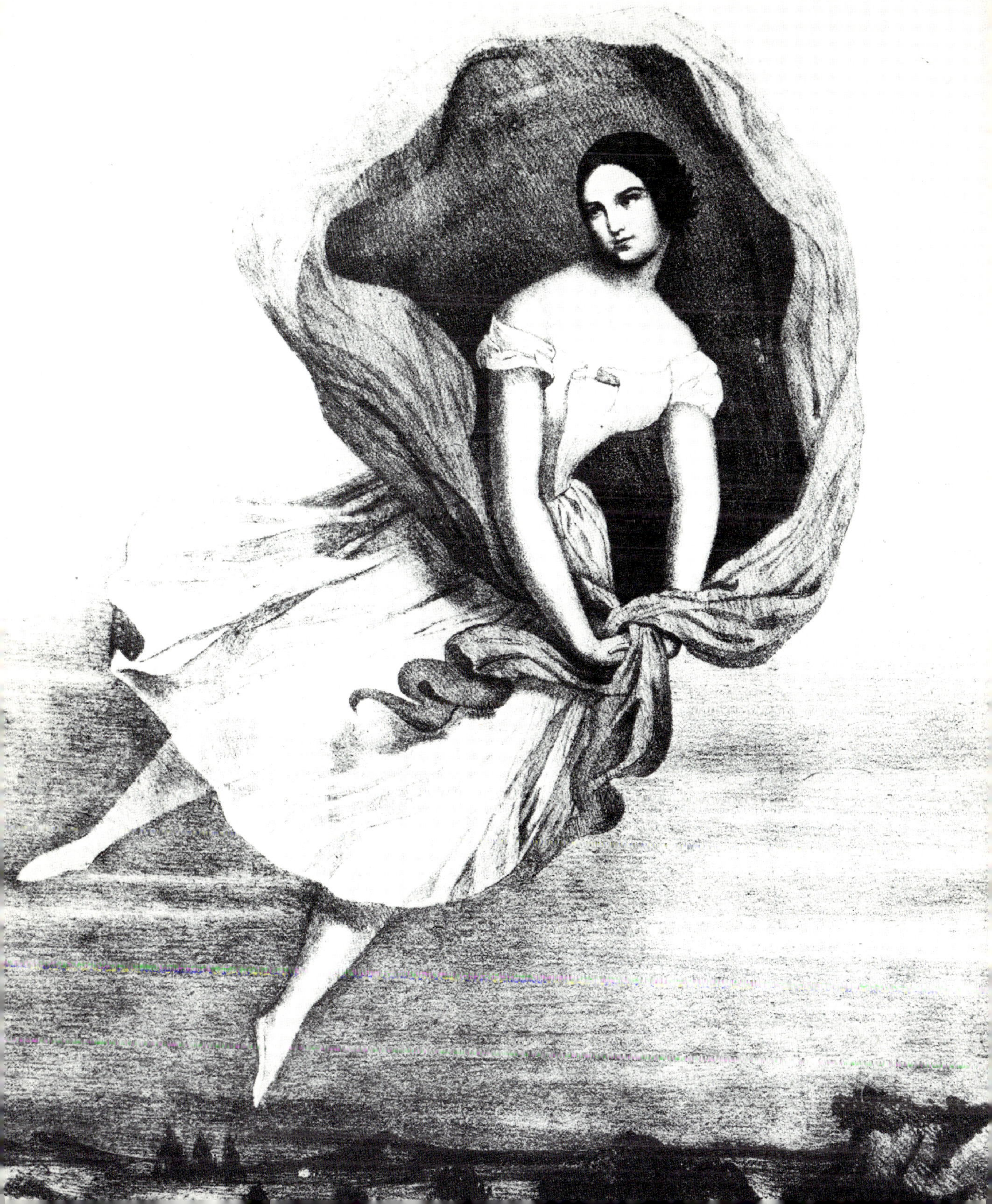

DANCE PERSPECTIVES FOUNDATION

Dance Perspectives Foundation was formed to encourage awareness and understanding of the art of dance as a great historical tradition and as a significant force in contemporary life. Believing that this aim can be furthered by literary activity, the Foundation is concerned to aid writers in undertaking studies on dance that will result in significant publications, to assist publishers in the selection and production of dance books, and to stimulate public interest in the finest dance literature.

Dance Perspectives Foundation has been ruled as exempt from Federal income tax by the United States Treasury Department, as an organization operated exclusively for educational purposes. Contributions, gifts and bequests to the Foundation are deductible from Federal income tax returns. Board of Directors: Selma Jeanne Cohen, president; Robert M. MacGregor, vice-president; Clive Barnes; J. R. de la Torre Bueno; Otis Cavrell; Martha Hill Davies; Natasha Deakin; Herbert Kummel; Thor Wood.

FOREWORD

In September, 1944, when *Dance Index* published George Chaffée's fourth and final catalogue of dance prints—"Three or Four Graces"—the editors remarked: "With this number *Dance Index* has listed over 1000 lithographs of the romantic ballet in Mr. Chaffée's catalogues, and the end is not yet. Next year we will present the catalogue of Italian entries...." How many print collectors and interested balletomanes have deplored the non-realization of that prediction! Now twenty-nine years later, with respectful recognition and gratitude to his illustrious, pioneering forebear, this author presents the Italian catalogue.

In addition to the crucial aid of my colleague collectors and to curators of public repositories, whose contribution is cited in the key to the catalogue and gratefully acknowledged herewith, I must also list debts of scholarship and friendship to the following persons: Maria Teresa Muraro of the Fondazione Giorgio Cini and Dr. Sandro della Libera of the Teatro della Fenice, Venice; Dr. Alessandro Piantanida, Enrico Vigevani and Otto Lorenzo of Milan; Mmes Gilberte Cournand, Marcelle Morillon and Sabine Zlatin, and Mlle Nicole Wild of Paris; Prof. Daniele Danieli of the Teatro San Carlo, Naples; Ivor Guest and John Hall of London; Katherine Gregory and Walter Schatzki of New York City.

There remains one special person whose chronological age (though not her spirit) has necessitated her retirement as curator of the Harvard Theatre Collection so that her name does not appear in the key to the catalogue. To redress this omission and restore her to a rightful place among those whose help was so necessary to this undertaking, I dedicate this monograph,

With much love and respectful admiration
to
Helen D. Willard who knew first.

EB3

INTRODUCTION

The Congress of Vienna in 1815 completely remade the map of Italy. That simple "geographical expression," as the Austrian chancellor Metternich labelled it when asked about the nationalistic aspirations for political unity, was re-fashioned to conform as closely as possible to the pre-Napoleonic *status quo*. The peninsula again became a patchwork of petty states with a few larger and stronger political entities. This political fragmentation is partly responsible for the rich diversity of the dance prints listed in the present catalogue. Whereas eleven Austrian and German cities account for the more than 470 prints in the period 1790-1890 (see *Dance Perspectives* 47), an incredible twenty-eight cities are responsible for a similar number of Italian prints for the period 1815-1875. Even more surprising is the fact that an additional six cities are known to have souvenirs in the form of eulogistic poems dedicated to ballet stars, even though prints have not yet been traced to them. This multitude of separate points of origin is not, however, entirely due to political complexity.

In the seventeenth and eighteenth centuries, a centralized France had a single *Académie royale de musique* while a very few provincial centers had semi-permanent lyric and dance troupes. In the Germanies, on the contrary, and to an even greater extent in Italy, there were numerous capital cities with permanent, resident companies capable of presenting the most complex operas and ballets.

Queen of the Italian opera houses was Milan's Teatro alla Scala, which presented its first ballet in its present building in 1778. Its nearest artistic rival was the San Carlo in Naples whose repertoire dated from 1737. The Teatro Regio of Turin claimed an ancestor in 1662, although political upheavals had caused several interruptions. The Fenice in Venice could not compete with her sisters in longevity but still boasted a first performance in 1792. In the smaller Italian capitals or former capitals, there were the Carlo Felice in Genoa, the Teatro della Pergola in Florence, and the Ducal Theatre in Parma. It was only in the capital of the Papal States, where religious ambivalence toward the stage in general and the dance in particular precluded the establishment of a permanent opera and ballet company, that a major Italian city did not present regular seasons by a regular troupe. Yet Rome did produce ballets at this time in three separate theatres: the Apollo, the Torre Argentina, and the Valle.

Still we are far from accounting for the total number of theatres responsible for dance prints. If Papal Rome had reservations about performances by scantily clad ballerinas, the other areas in the States of the Church had no such qualms. Ancona, Bologna, Cesena, Faenza, Ferrara, Perugia, Ravenna, and Senigallia all welcomed dancers at various times and published souvenir prints to memorialize their visits. La Fenice did nothing to minimize seasons in Venetian Padua, Rovigo, Verona or Vicenza, any more than did la Scala for Lombard Brescia and Como, or the Pergola in Florence for Tuscan Leghorn, Pisa, and Pistoia. Even the tiny states of Parma and Modena saw ballet in other towns beside the two capital cities, while Italian-speaking Trieste in Istria, despite its inclusion in the Austrian Empire until 1918, still provides a small section of our catalogue. (Non-existent or destroyed theatre archives explain many *lacunae,* and the complete lack of entries from the major city of Palermo.)

There is yet another reason for the proliferation of Italian dance prints: the dual conception of the role of the print itself. Any theatrical souvenir fulfils two functions: first, it is a tribute to the performer who is recognized by it; second, it is the spectators' memento of the performance. The dance print normally assumes both roles, but certain designs are closer to one or the other of them. Consider the beautifully hand-colored London ballet lithographs, showing a dancer in a particular role, sometimes labelled "proof" to indicate that they are the finest examples of those pulled from the stone or plate. They usually bear a date of publication shortly after the date of the premiere performance. They were printed with great care on beautiful, heavy paper. They were meant to be treasured for a long time. Their *raison d'être* was to be saved—either framed or in an album—to remind their owner of an evening at the theatre.

The typical Italian dance print most often belongs to the other category. Its paper is never of the heavy, durable variety; it is almost never colored. It is often accompanied by a dedicatory verse (even to the use of "D.D.D." meaning "the dedicators" or "Gli Ammiratori"—"the admirers"), and it frequently appears that little care was spent on its printing. It is a more spontaneous production—and for a simple reason. It is primarily a tribute to the dancer depicted. Obvious are the thin paper used, as well as the apparent speed of production which caused wholesale pirating of existing likenesses and explains the numerous variants in the catalogue. Sometimes the original artist of a portrait is remembered on subsequent printings. Most often he is not. Frequently the new artist who "copied" or "adapted" an existing likeness used his own name. Sometimes, however, he remained anonymous, with becoming modesty because of the poor quality of his work.

The quickness of the prints' production mirrored the speed of the dancer who had to travel from city to city for closely timed engagements. The sheet in honor of the performer was distributed in the theatre during the performance. Italian dedicatory poems and prints were more intimately connected with the local opera houses than were their English counterparts. This probably accounts, not only for their frequent sketchiness, but also for their rarity. It can also explain the two different states of many of the prints: the more common on thin, plain paper for the single occasion; the others on tinted paper for the collector's album.

The history of the Italian dance print before 1800 is not easy to establish because of the paucity of known examples. A group of four similar Milanese engravings of three different ballerinas sheds some light on the problem. They are lavish and complex—measuring almost twenty-one inches in height by fifteen in width. Earliest in date is one dedicated to Anna Sabbatini "che con arte, grazia mirabile balla nel Reg. Duc. Teatro in Milano per la famosa opera del 1746." (A/B 3943. Repr: F/A II, p. 157). Two years later, the same artist, Marc'Antonio Dal Re (1697-1766), designed a companion work of the same dancer as she performed on the same stage during the carnival season of 1748. Dal Re apparently waited thirteen years before making additional souvenir prints. He then commemorated the similar carnival appearances of Lucia Fabris (A/B 1476. Repr: A/B Tav. V, opp. p. 96, and F/A II, p. 153). In that same year, Gerolamo Cattaneo immortalized the "inpareggiabile" Santina Zanuzzi (A/B 4772; IG, Romb 20. Repr: Carr p. 33 and, bottom section only, E/S III, p. 1196). Each of these presents a laudatory sonnet, and three show a bust or half-length portrait of the dancer. In addition, each contains a vignette of the performer in a scene on stage, usually with a partner. These souvenirs are

9

ALL' INCOMPARABILE SIGNORA
ANNA SABATINI BOLOGNESE
DANZANDO CON UNIVERSALE APPLAUSO NEL REGIO DUCAL TEATRO DI MILANO IL CARNOVALE DELL' ANNO 1748

Sonetto

Anna qualor tu rustica, e negletta
Ninfa sembri di Lago, o pur di Balza,
Che armoniosi alterni colpi affretta,
E per l'aere or vola, e in terra or balza:

Non così vigorosa onda ristretta
Da piombato canal se stessa incalza,
Ne lo sguardo così ferma, ed alletta
Mentre varia, e leggiera al Ciel s'innalza.

Piaci, ma turbi insiem gli occhi bramosi,
Che intenti al lusinghier viso giocondo
Tanti perdon de tuoi passi ingegnosi.

Io ti seguo cò plausi, e mi confondo,
Son sì rapidi i tuoi salti vezzosi
Che lodando il primier lodo il secondo.

extremely lavish and complex. They were obviously meant to be saved.

Of almost comparable complexity were the large sheets of eulogistic poems; these, however, without figural representation of the ballerina. The one that frames the foreword to this issue is dedicated to Maria Teresa Campioni who performed the heroine in the ballet *Alonso e Cora* at the "Nobilissimo Teatro di San Benedetto" (precursor of la Fenice) in Venice in 1783. Of equal ornamental charm are prints of an otherwise unknown Teresa Zambelli, dancing in a wooded glade, and of the ballet master Jean-Baptiste Martin, who worked in Venice between 1760 and 1784. His half-length portrait "entro cornice architettonica" (A/B 2703) bears the name of Denis Valesi, who dedicated it to him. For Zambelli, however, no other information—neither artists' names, nor place, nor date of publication are there for supplemental identification. (It is possible that this print bears some relation to another likeness of Zambelli by Giuseppe Camerata [1718-1803] which includes eight verses. A copy exists in the Graphiksammlung of the Historisches Museum der Stadt Wien.)

With these extremely rare examples, we are left to reconstruct the history of Italian dance prints before about 1790. One thing is clear. The large, lavish engravings were not produced frequently. They were too big and too complex for easy distribution in the opera houses. The last decade of the eighteenth century and the beginning of the nineteenth produced a solution: the complicated frame was omitted. If a laudatory sonnet was desired along with a portrait of the dancer, the two were printed on opposite halves of a folded sheet. This arrangement appears in prints of Antonio Muzzarelli dated 1790 (A/B 3040), of Domenico Serpos performing at the Torre Argentina in 1796 (A/B 4146) and of Teresa Luzzi early in the new century (A/B 2464). The last example of the folded sheet appears for the choreographer Gaspare Ronzi at the Torre Argentina in 1813 (A/B 3777). All four examples are from Rome.

Many of the smaller prints of the late eighteenth and early nineteenth century also included poetry. Contemporary examples often fail to list even the designer's or engraver's name. Luigia Zerbi (A/B 4779), Onorato Viganò, father of the greatest Italian choreographer at the beginning of the period, and Michele Fabiani (A/B 1470) are cases in point. Fabiani is shown in an amusing variant of the last-named print. His ballets at the Torre Argentina in Rome during the carnival season 1791 did not satisfy all of the local balletomanes. At least one of them attested his displeasure by commissioning a likeness taken from the existing print—but with the dancer decapitated and with an ass's head lying beside him (A/B 1471). A lovely, full-length oval of Teresa Monticini, in the Dance Collection of The New York Public Library, comes from Trieste in 1803 (see note to no. 62). A renowned mime at la Scala from 1800-1807, Monticini was Mistress of Mime in the ballet school there from the late 1820's.

Teresa Zambelli

Anna Sabbatini

Michele Fabiani

In 1815 the Italian dance scene was dominated by a group of personalities whom the Romantic Ballet was to know as choreographers and ballet masters rather than as performers. Most famous was Salvatore Viganò, whose early fame as a leading dancer had paled before his greater talents as a choreographer. His listings here of ten separate numbers and three variants reflect these later gifts; none show him dancing (no. 436). The series of his great ballets at la Scala had just begun with *Gli Strelitzi* (December 26, 1811) although he had previously choreographed works in Venice and Vienna. They were to continue until his death ten years later: *il Noce di Benevento* ("ottimo"), *l'Alunno della giumenta* ("buonissimo"), *Prometeo* ("ottimo"), *il Nuovo Pigmalione* (the same), *Numa Pompilio* ("buonissimo"), *Psammi re d'Egitto* (the same), *Otello* after Shakespeare ("ottimo"), *la Vestale* (the same, with forty performances), and *Alessandro nelle Indie* (again "buonissimo"—these comments from Cambiasi, pp. 370-373), among others.

We are fortunate in having a large group of aquatints showing sets for these productions along with many others by the talented Alessandro Sanquirico (1777-1849). A scenery-designer at la Scala beginning in 1806, Sanquirico was responsible for all productions there from 1817 to 1832. It is unfortunate, however, that we have no pictorial records of the costumes worn in these works. Our earliest group of costume plates (series A), those for *Guidone Selvaggio ossia le guerriere d'Alessandra* (April 15, 1816), was considered worthy to be issued as the second *fascicule* in the *Fasti del Regio Teatro alla Scala di Milano* along with Mozart's *il Flauto magico* and Rossini's *l'Inganno felice*. The *Fasti* of the title were connected with the visit of the Emperor Francis I with his wife and mother to Milan for his coronation. The leading dancers in *Guidone Selvaggio* were Antonietta Millier and Caterino Titus (no. 275). Unfortunately, the ballet was not one of Viganò's. It was by Giorza and was labelled "cattivo."

No. 436. Salvatore Viganò

No. 275. Antonietta Millier and Caterino Titus

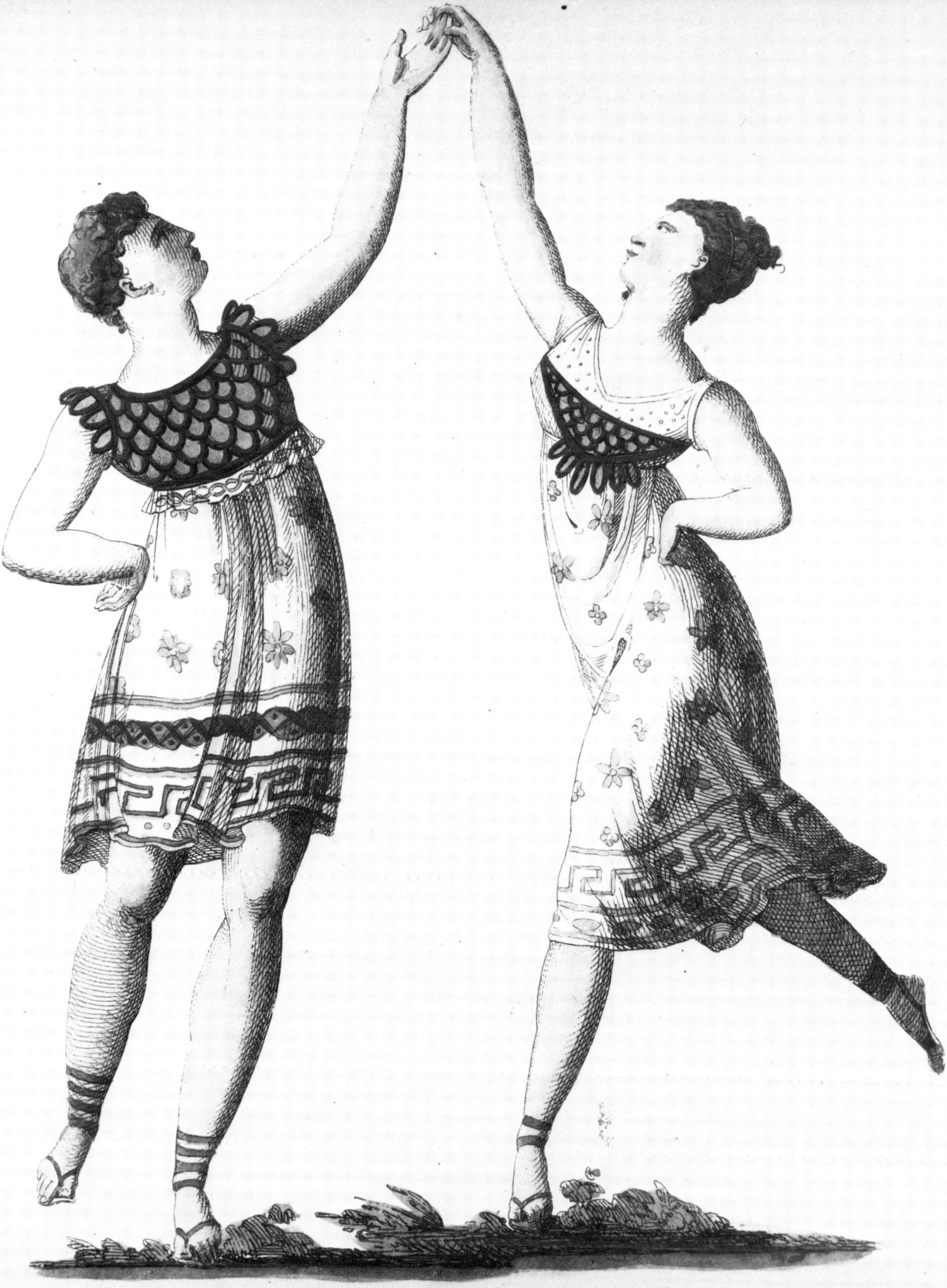

If Viganò is not presented as a performer, neither is his almost exact contemporary, Gaetano Gioja. Even while serving as leading dancer, he choreographed his first ballets—in Milan during the carnival season of 1794 and in Naples from 1803. His bust, along with that of his dancer-choreographer brother Ferdinando, probably antedates the beginning year of this catalogue, but provides a good bridge between the earlier engravings and the later lithographs (no. 112).

Also shortly before our starting date is a pair of companion medals showing Giovanni and Teresa Coralli in 1813 (no. 69). A native Bolognese, married to a Frenchwoman from Bordeaux, Giovanni became better known as Jean in Paris where he appeared first at the Porte-Saint-Martin (1825-31) and later at the Opéra (1831-50). To consider him only as the leading ballet master of the Romantic period in France is to forget the *premier danseur* of London (1803), Vienna (1806-07) and Italy.

Other choreographers still performing as dancers about 1815 include Armand Vestris, son and grandson of Italian-born stars who made their fame and fortune in Paris and London. Armand returned to Naples as leading dancer and choreographer before his early death while ballet master in Vienna (no. 443). There was also the French Louis (Luigi) Henry who danced longest in Naples, but also in Milan and Vienna, before beginning a career as choreographer at la Scala, Naples and Vienna. Not welcomed warmly at the Opéra where he designed a ballet for Fanny Elssler, he ended his career in Paris with the extravaganza *Chao Kang* at the Théâtre Nautique.

If we have found no Italian prints of Filippo Taglioni, teacher and choreographer for his daughter Marie, such is not the case with his younger brother Salvatore. While Filippo danced at la Scala in 1813 and in Turin in 1815 before he embarked on a peripatetic life that ranged from Paris to Russia, Salvatore, with his wife Adelaide Taglioni-Peraud, settled almost permanently in Naples. The season 1812-13 witnessed his debut there. It was then that he, along with Luigi Henry, who was also performing there, opened the Ballet School of the Royal Theatres—the San Carlo and the Teatro del Fondo. Two years later Salvatore's future wife made her debut in Naples. They were still there in the 1850's and 1860's. As early as 1816, Taglioni's students at the ballet school dedicated a print to him. Twenty-two years later, his newest ballet *Faust* opened the Neapolitan carnival season 1838-39. It was his ninety-sixth work! (no. 237). His daughter Luisina is also remembered from Naples in one of the most charming prints of our gallery (no. 231). She later danced for nine seasons at the Opéra in Paris (1848-57).

Slightly younger than these ballet masters and choreographers but the only one who can remotely compare with Viganò in his number of published Italian prints, Carlo Blasis is best known as a teacher. His debut as *premier danseur* in Milan occurred during the carnival season of 1818, although his dancing ca-

No. 112. Gaetano and Ferdinando Gioja

No. 69. Giovanni and Teresa Coralli

reer had started when he was twelve. Even before he became master of the class of "perfezionamento" at the school of la Scala in the middle 1830's, he had published two major books: *The Treatise on the Dance* (1820) and *The Code of Terpsichore* (1830). He is supposedly responsible for the pose called "attitude," a balletic interpretation of the statue of Mercury by Giovanni da Bologna (1524-1608). With his wife, Annunziata Ramaccini, as teaching partner, Blasis was responsible for the training of a generation of students including the preferred seven he called his "Pleiades." He is represented here by a marble bust surrounded by an ornamental frame depicting the most favored of his prize students, Marietta Baderna (no. 16).

The ballets invented by the Italian choreographers, and by others who were no less prolific for not leaving portraits, were very different from the works of today, or even from those usual in France at the same time. The typical ballet at the Paris Opéra was a dance

No. 113. Armand Vestris

No. 231. Luisina Taglioni and Eugenio Durand

No. 237. Salvatore Taglioni

No. 16. Var. Carlo Blasis

drama in which the leading roles were performed by the leading dancers. Hence a *premier danseur* or ballerina both mimed a role and danced it. In Italy this was not the fashion. The work labelled a "ballo" was a mimo-drama, often on a major historical theme, with a complex plot of several acts—often as many as four or five—which made an entire evening's program. (In France, a ballet in one, two or three acts shared the bill with a short opera.) The leading performers in these "balli" were called "ballerini per le parte." They interpreted their long, involved roles with a series of stylized gestures, executed on the beat of the music. Their histrionic abilities were not remotely hampered by their muteness. In fact, the native Italian exuberance, or extroversion, may well have given rise to this style. The "primi ballerini," the leading dancing dancers, appeared in these works in divertissements or *ballabile* that frequently had little or nothing to do

No. 167. Antonietta Pallerini

No. 206. Domenico Ronzani and Francesca Pezzoli

No. 50. Fanny Cerrito

with the plots of the ballets. In any season at any of the Italian opera houses, there was a *prima mima assoluta,* with male partner and subsidiary colleagues, as well as a *prima ballerina assoluta* with her partner and colleagues.

Of the great mimes none was more famous than Antonietta Pallerini, whose professional career at la Scala extended from 1813 to 1840. Her importance to the Italian ballet scene is attested by the fact that she merits fifteen of our prints, a larger number than any other performer except Fanny Cerrito. Her constant partner was Nicola Molinari whose printed souvenirs (eleven) better the record of any other male dancer-choreographer except Viganò.

The art of the mimes is only suggested by the prints (nos. 167, 206). Great talent was an obvious trait of these performers. Another was longevity. Age ended most of the ballerina's careers, but youth was not a prerequisite for their actor-colleagues to whom experience was much more important. Many former leading dancers "graduated" to mimed roles when their technical supremacy waned, just as some became choreographers or ballet masters. Taglioni performed as leading dancer twenty-five years (1822-47), Elssler twenty-four (1827-51), Grisi twenty-four (1829-53). In contrast, it is not surprising that several of Pallerini's and Molinari's fellow mimes had unusually long careers. Giuseppe Bocci, who was already performing by 1816 (*Guidone Selvaggio,* and probably earlier), was still miming at la Scala in 1861. Effizio Catte (active at least between 1827-63) and Pietro Trigambi (at least 1816-61) were other long-lived performers.

Foremost of the international stars in Italy was Fanny Cerrito who, unlike most of her rivals, won her place in that gallery in her homeland before making her foreign conquests. The first dated print recalls her triumphs in Turin at the Teatro Carignano in autumn, 1835, and in carnival 1835-36 at the more important Teatro Regio. After two short seasons in Turin and others in Vienna, she became an almost permanent member of the ballet troupe at la Scala. We have a print of her as Fenella in Auber's opera *la Muta di Portici,* which she first performed there on December 26, 1838 (no. 50). Between her seasons in Milan, Cerrito made short appearances in Brescia and Vicenza, each of which issued a poem surrounded by an ornamental frame. The one from Vicenza (1839)

No. 119. Carlotta Grisi

provides the cover for this issue (no. 51). In 1840 Cerrito left Italy to begin to assume her position as a world-famous performer with the first of her many seasons in London. In subsequent tours of her homeland, she was an international star rather than a native dancer.

A native of the Italian-speaking province of Istria in the Austrian Empire, Carlotta Grisi studied at the school of la Scala before beginning to perform elsewhere in the peninsula. She and Cerrito both danced in Florence and in Naples during 1833-34. They even performed a *pas de cinq* together in one of Salvatore Taglioni's innumerable ballets at the San Carlo (November 14, 1834). Their paths crossed again in Vienna during carnival, 1836-37. Grisi had now met and begun a love affair with the great French dancer Jules Perrot. Carlotta may have staked the first claim to Perrot's person, but Fanny greatly profited by his teaching during this first Viennese visit. A projected *pas de deux* for the two rivals during the Coronation season at la Scala (autumn, 1838) had not materialized because of mutual jealousy, and, while Fanny continued at la Scala, Carlotta furthered her training with Perrot which soon resulted in a Paris season at the Théâtre de la Renaissance and eventual *première danseuse* status at the Opéra, clinched by the huge success of *Giselle* there in 1841. Unlike Cerrito, who continued to perform part of nearly every year in Italy until 1848, Carlotta was content with her Parisian position and frequent seasons in London. While prints of Cerrito poured from Italian presses in each new city—including a pirated version of a lovely London souvenir originally showing her in *le Lac des Fées*, now called *Aglaija ossia il Lago delle Fate* (no. 55)—it was not until the carnival season of 1846-47 at the Teatro Apollo in Rome that Grisi finally reappeared in the peninsula. This single Roman season is remembered by a pose from the *pas de Diane* in *la Jolie Fille de Gand,* another of her Paris triumphs (no. 119). Carlotta did not dance again in Italy.

The third great international star who danced in Naples before achieving world-wide fame was Fanny Elssler. She was the most assiduous of the touring ballerinas from abroad. After an initial visit to la Scala during carnival, 1837-38, just before Cerrito's many successive seasons there, she returned to Italy continuously from December, 1844, to February, 1848. Her half-length portrait of 1845 by the Austrian Kriehuber (Germ 70) accompanied her everywhere (no. 84). Variants of it are found from Rome as well

No. 84 Var. A. Fanny Elssler

No. 83. Fanny Elssler

as from Bologna and Ancona. Little Senigallia, however, preferred greater originality, using an Italian music cover instead of the Kriehuber portrait. Its charming souvenir shows Elssler, the greatest actress-dancer of the stars, in a relaxed arabesque in Perrot's *Esmeralda*, which he had choreographed especially for her in London (March 9, 1844) and which she danced at la Scala the following December (no. 83). (It was banned later during performances in Rome, since the villain was a monk.) Elssler's Italian triumphs ended in bitterness. La Scala witnessed the Italian premiere of Perrot's *Faust* on February 12, 1848, when counter-Austrian propaganda was at its height and revolution was only a few months away. The Viennese Fanny was greeted by whistles in an only partly filled house. She departed, never to dance in Italy again.

Marie Taglioni was half Italian, but she apparently felt no need to visit her uncle's family in Naples. She did, however, realize that triumphs were as financially sound in the peninsula as elsewhere. During a single month in 1841 she performed eight times at la Scala. Milan already knew her greatest vehicle *la Sylphide*, which she had presented all over Europe. Cerrito had appeared in an adaptation of it the previous January and was no doubt still remembered for the print that showed her holding the bird's nest in the second act. The older star was drawn by Roberto Focosi in her other ballet of this first Italian tour, *la Gitana* (no. 232). When Taglioni reappeared at la Scala, again for a single month the next year, prices were doubled to make up the huge sum demanded for her performances. In Bologna, during the autumn of 1842, she danced in another ballet from her Paris seasons, *la Fille du Danube*. Her portrait by the Bolognese A. Frulli was published at this time (no. 234). In Rome, her visit of 1846 was immortalized by the lithographer Roscioni's coarse adaptation of a London portrait by Edwin D. Smith, showing her with a small dog in her lap.

Taglioni appeared in Italy only after her reputation had become legendary. Lucile Grahn similarly performed in Italy as she danced across Europe, finally settling in Munich. Two years after her Milanese performances of 1843-44, the *Strenna teatrale*—one of the innumerable little theatrical almanachs of the period—published a variant of an early Danish likeness as previously adapted in Paris to commemorate

No. 234. Marie Taglioni

her dancing at the Opéra. The prolific Battistelli in Rome also designed a version of the English John Brandard's print (Eng 71) showing her as Catarina in Perrot's London ballet which the great choreographer later revived for Elssler at la Scala (January 9, 1847). (The same print was used as basis for German and Austrian prints of Grahn—see Germ 107-109 and 443; Sofia Fuoco in the same ballet in a similar pose appears in a Spanish version.)

Several non-Italians remained long enough in Italy to influence the dance scene and merit printed souvenirs. Elise Vaque-Moulin was one of the early ballerinas who experimented with dancing *sur les pointes*. She performed in Italy from the early 1820's to the mid 1830's. Other Frenchwomen were Antoinette Dupain, Thérèse (Teresa) Héberlé, and Angelica Saint-Romain. Their male counterparts were Jean Rozier, Antoine Paul, leading male dancer at the Opéra, and Auguste Lefebvre. The loveliest souvenir of these French expatriates was issued for the benefit performance of Adélaïde Mersy and Jean Rousset at the Teatro della Pergola in Florence on May 19, 1828 (no. 156). It shows that acrobatic feats like the lifting of the dancer by her male partner did not have to show any physical strain, just as Taglioni was showing the aesthetic potentialities of the *danse sur les pointes*.

Other non-Italians of a later period included Nathalie FitzJames, who danced throughout the peninsula after a not remarkably brilliant career at the Paris Opéra. She is remembered as the first Giselle in Genoa, Florence and Naples. François Mérante and his wife Adélaïde were portrayed by the Neapolitan artist Luigi DeCrescenzo, who similarly honored six other performers at the San Carlo, including FitzJames, Amalia Ferraris, Amina Boschetti and Salvatore Taglioni.

An even more famous male dancer was the prodigious Arthur Saint-Léon, continuous partner of Fanny Cerrito after their marriage on April 17, 1845. They had just completed a carnival season in Rome where each merited a print. Now the virtuoso violinist, best remembered as choreographer of *Coppélia*, drew his own self-portrait, a unique example of a dance print also designed by its sitter (no. 222).

No. 222. Arthur Saint-Léon

No. 130. Adélaïde Mersy and Jean Rousset

Of all the foreign dancers who performed in Italy and remained there, none was more important than Augusta Maywood. Her amazing career, which started with a debut as a child prodigy in Philadelphia, has already tempted two of our collector-colleagues. Marian Hannah Winter's excellent article in *Dance Index* traced the major stages in Maywood's career, in Paris, Lisbon, and Vienna, concluding with residence in Italy and continuous itinerant performing. Besides reproducing four prints of the ballerina, Miss Winter pioneered in the field of iconography, listing a total of thirteen likenesses, including eight Italian prints. Parmenia Migel also wrote on Maywood in *The Ballerinas*. Rather than reproduce familiar pictures—and despite our admiration for the lovely example showing a bewigged Rita Gauthier in a ballet adaptation of *la Dame aux Camélias*—we have chosen a dancing pose from Padua in 1851 (no. 142) and a portrait souvenir from an undated season in Trieste (no. 144). Both are unique, existing in only one of the collections examined for the catalogue. Our third selection presents a full-length costume print from a Turin series dated 1857. Although figuring in the Winter iconography (no. 12), it also has never been previously reproduced (no. 460).

We must now turn to the native-born, whose major artistic concern was apparently to succeed enough in Italy to embark on international careers like Cerrito's. Foremost of these were the "Pleiades," the seven favorite students of Carlo Blasis. Augusta Dominechettis is not represented by printed portraits. Carolina Granzini, Marietta Baderna, and Pasquale Borri, the lone *danseur* among them, had only one each. Borri, who became a renowned choreographer, had toured extensively as partner-husband of Carolina Pochini, who merited a number of prints.

The date of birth of the Florentine Flora Fabbri is not known, but she was already ballerina in Rome at carnival, 1843. We see her as la Sylphide in a Roman souvenir of that early season (no. 86), and with her husband Luigi Bretin in *la Zingarella* from later the same year (no. 33). She became better known shortly afterwards as leading dancer at the Opéra (1845-51) and in London (1845-46, 1848) as well as in Germany. Of the Pleiades, she was the first to achieve international recognition.

No. 142. Augusta Maywood

No. 144. Augusta Maywood

No. 86. Flora Fabbri

No. 460. Augusta Maywood

The year 1843 was important also for other Blasis pupils. After a carnival-lent at la Scala in which Cerrito danced the first Italian production of *Giselle* and Marie Taglioni also appeared, there were three short seasons that featured dancers trained by the great teacher. In the spring it was Giovannina King. Although not one of the favored "Pleiades," she had already appeared in several seasons at Milan alongside Cerrito or Taglioni. Her omission from the select seven may have been due to her Neapolitan birth and earlier training under Pietro Hus and Gustavo Carey. Three prints show her arabesque: one from Mantua in 1843 (no. 133), a second from Rome in 1844 (no. 134), and a variant of the first, probably for one of her several Scala seasons (no. 439). After 1847, she seems to have disappeared.

In 1843 la Scala held a short series of summer performances, presenting the professional debut of the thirteen-year-old Sofia Fuoco. Maria Brambilla chose "Sofia" to go with the Italian word for "fire," the surname she had assumed previously—an apt choice. Her technique was faultless—*pointes* "like steel arrows rebounding from a marble pavement," wrote Théophile Gautier about her Paris debut three years later. She is reported to have been the first to execute unsupported pirouettes on full *pointes,* an exceptional feat in the unblocked toe shoes of the day. After seasons in Paris and London, she returned to tour various Italian cities between 1850 and 1857. Florence remembered her in a tarantella within a floral oval. This beautiful print obscures the fact that she was extremely homely. Modenese and Faentine artists flattered her less than the Florentine ones (no. 105).

The last great member of Blasis's Pleiades was the famous Amalia Ferraris. Possessed of a technique as strong as Fuoco's, she was apparently an even better jumper. Chaffée labels her "the mistress of the *entrechat-huit.*" Her adoring husband, sending a telegram to the Director of the Paris Opéra, waxed even more eloquent. "Diva balladiera" was his ecstatic description, as he recounted the number of times she was recalled for additional bows at the end of her performance in Bologna (Goncourt *Journal,* II, p. 168– October 26, 1857). She performed all over Italy before dancing in London, Paris, and St. Petersburg. Cyril Beaumont included a marvellous print, the only

No. 134. Giovannina King

No. 105. Sofia Fuoco

Italian example in his lavish catalogue; but he misattributed it to Battistelli in Rome, although it lists Genoa, 1849, in is title. We reproduce an even rarer example that conveys the admirable *ballon* Ferraris could obviously command (no. 433).

Some great contemporary dancers did not receive their la Scala training under Blasis. Amalia Brugnoli had studied there from about 1817. An early exponent of *pointe* work, she is best remembered by two Viennese prints showing the earliest examples of an arabesque supported by a partner and of a "lift" (Germ 17 and 20). The second of these is four years previous to the Italian one of Adélaïde Mersy and Jean Rousset (no. 156). Along with her husband, Paolo Samengo, Brugnoli performed at la Scala, la Fenice, and the San Carlo as well as in London during the 1820's and 1830's. After the souvenirs of their British season in 1832, the later prints are all Italian, including the single example of a ballerina included in the twelve plates issued to commemorate the reopening of la Fenice for carnival, 1837-38 (series Q). Brugnoli's last season, in Rome in 1840, is remembered by a full-length print (no. 37). In her day she had been a unique performer, but younger rivals were already supplanting their elders.

The two Roman carnival seasons after Brugnoli's retirement presented the young Carolina Galletti. A first print from Turin dated 1838, when she was only twelve, seems very early, but she had already danced at Verona at the age of ten. Another print was published in Rome in 1841 and reissued the next year no. 109). After her marriage to the dancer Fran-

No. 433. Amalia Ferraris

No. 37. Amalia Brugnoli

cesco Rosati, she was billed as "Galletti-Rosati," but she later dropped her maiden name entirely to become a formidable "Madame Rosati" for six seasons in Paris, first as rival of Cerrito and later of Ferraris. Although not as strong a technician as the Blasis-trained Ferraris, she was superior as a dramatic actress. The enormous success at the Opéra in 1856 of Adolphe Adam's last ballet *le Corsaire,* which starred Rosati, was such that even an Italian print commemorated its vogue (no. 110). She had been the only ballerina beside the sacrosanct Marie Taglioni to perform the *Pas de Quatre* in both London and Milan. When she left Paris in 1859, she stopped dancing.

Carolina Pochini has already been mentioned as the wife of the dancer-choreographer Pasquale Borri. Her name, like that of Fuoco and Rosati, was changed at the beginning of her career. One of her earliest seasons in 1852 occasioned a print which listed her as Carlotta Ranieri Pochini. A likeness from Milan in the spring of 1855 is dedicated to "Carolina" although her facsimile signature reads "Carlotta" (no. 187). She thereafter must have bowed to the inevitable and accepted the name we recognize. The greatest part she created, one she first performed in Turin during the 1866-67 season, was the leading role in her husband's ballet *Idea.* Turin knew three different prints of her in this work (no. 189).

No. 187. Carolina Pocchini

No. 109. Carolina Galletti-Rosati

Amina Boschetti was the last of the great Italian ballerinas to be well represented in prints. Her artistry was not much appreciated at the Paris Opéra where she was nicknamed "Malagamba" when she created *la Maschera* (1864). So she returned to Naples where she certainly was loved. The *pas de quatre* from the ballet *Folgore* at the San Carlo in 1861 is delightful (no. 21). Three other prints testify to many Neapolitan admirers; one shows a determined woman in peasant costume (no. 22).

Italian series of dance prints are not as numerous as those of France, England or the Germanies and Austria. Although a large number of Italian cities published individual portraits, only four could sustain the expenditure of continued publication. Milan, as the largest political capital and home of la Scala, can be automatically awarded pride of place. In Italy, then as now, the industrial north was more wealthy and more enterprising. Venice, Turin and Milan account for all but two groups, with a few subsidiary prints coming from Naples. One of these two Neapolitan series, the only Italian costume prints to follow the lead of the hundreds of Martinet engravings from Paris, is constituted from only two examples (series L). We know neither the general title, length of publication, nor other examples than the two mentioned in the catalogue.

Considerably later is a larger group of eleven portraits of dancers, not all of whom even performed in Naples (series M). Between 1839 and 1844 a newspaper called *la Poliorama pittoresca* issued a short appendix entitled *la Moda*. In addition to a colored fashion plate *hors-texte*, each issue contained a portrait of a celebrity with a biography. It is indicative of the dance interest of the publishers that Marie Taglioni appeared in the first issue. Five years later, eleven dancers had been so honored.

Venice's contribution to the series consists of a single almanach (series P) and a later, larger souvenir (series Q). The reopening of la Fenice for carnival-lent 1837-38, after a fire which had closed the theatre for a year, was heralded by a lovely volume. We know of two complete copies of the *Dodici principali artisti*. The Scala one has conventional binding. Madame de Moroda's is bound in pale blue with Empire-style decoration of antique masks, sheaves of musical trophies, and an eagle above a flaming dish. The same devices were featured on the separate plates by the lithographer Barozzi after the designs of the artist Eugenio Napoleone Pianta. Along with eight singers the volume features Amalia Brugnoli, Antonio Cortesi, Domenico Mattis (no. 464), and Antonio Ramacini. With the exception of the presentation copies of Sanquirico's acquatinted stage designs and illustrated book souvenirs of certain Savoyard royal tournaments in Turin, no other Italian theatrical souvenir is more elegant or lavish.

Turin also produced two series—each one part of a newspaper. The *Galleria teatrale* of 1856 and 1857 (series O) featured three dancers: Catarina Beretta, Boschetti, and Maywood. Another Turin series, probably slightly earlier, appeared in the newspaper *le Scintille-Gazzetta della Sera* (series N).

All other known series of Italian dance prints come from Milan and are closely connected with la Scala or its subsidiary theatre the Canobbiana. There are memorial souvenirs of a single season, groups from theatrical newspapers, collections of portraits, and a magnificent run of yearly almanachs dating from 1822 to 1836. In addition, there is a series of at least eighty-one costume plates from five separate ballets produced at la Scala between 1827 and 1831. They are by three different choreographers: Henry, Galzerani, and Horschelt.

No. 189. Carolina Pochini

No. 21. Amina Boschetti

Chronologically first among the Milanese series is the ballet *Guidone Selvaggio* section of the *Fasti* of 1816 (series A). Next come the twelve dance personalities included in the *Raccolta di 96 retratti di musicisti ed artisti di teatro* published by the prolific Giorgio Ricordi in 1821 (series B). Luigi Rados, who engraved the small bust portraits of the dancers, placed them on dark backgrounds with texts below. The likenesses are certainly excellent when compared to other portraits of the same worthies, but nothing beside their names and the explanations below suggest anything of their profession. Another group of portraits, the eight busts of *la Tersicore milanese* (also dating from 1821), were published by the Vallardis (series C). Again, without the names and the poems accompanying each bust in the complete volume, no one would guess the sitters' occupation. The third set of bust portraits comes from what must have been an extremely large series, since the three prints that bear numbers fall in the 580's. Inability to find a complete edition to check, as well as the presence of unnumbered plates, forces us to list the dancers alphabetically (series D).

Without the fortuitous preservation in a Venetian library of two bound collections of Milanese costume plates, the few scattered examples from the same series in other locations could never have allowed even sketchy cataloguing. The Biblioteca Marciana is not notably interested in theatre and dance, but there it is possible at least to trace the complexity of the only known two series of Italian dance costumes. One is entitled *Raccolta di Figurini ad uso dei teatri— Giusta il costum de tutti tempi e di tutti le nazioni* (series E). It was published in Milan by the *incizione* Stucchi who was even then issuing the designs by Sanquirico. The didactic idea of the publisher was to portray "every epoch" and "every nation." Among the American, Chinese, Egyptian, French, Crusader, and other series of costumes were individual plates of dance interest, but such a motley group could

No. 464. Domenico Mattis

No. 22. Amina Boschetti

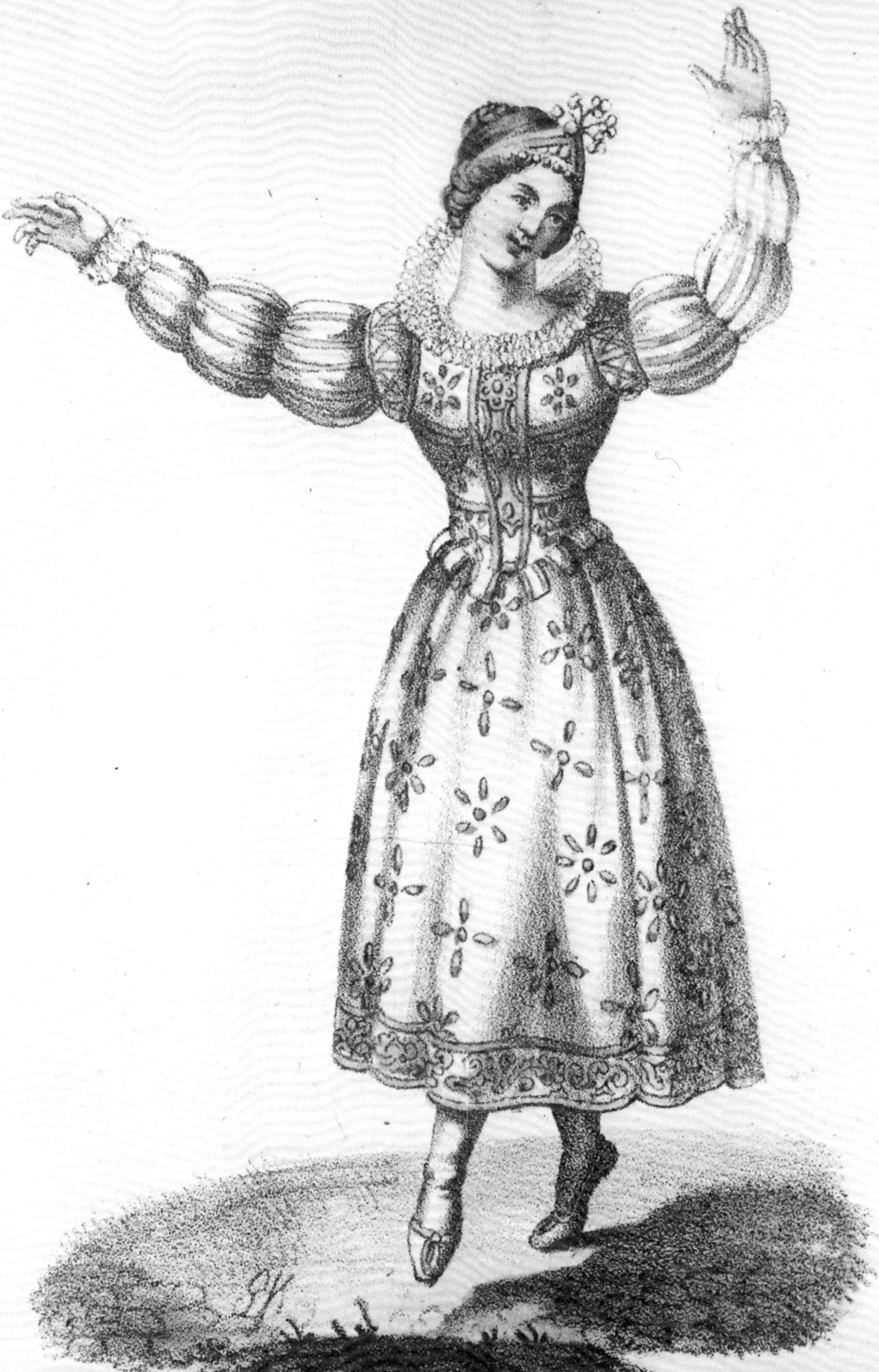

No. 387. "Damigelle" from *la Vedova nel giorno delle nozze*

No. 405. Teresa Héberlé

never have been issued purely as a theatrical souvenir.

The other volume at the Marciana is better systematized but even less definite of title (series F). Its binding bears the notation *Collezione di Figuri Teatrali,* but this may have been merely the suggestion to a binder by the former owner of the individual illustrations. A number of the plates are those of the preceding collection. There are also, however, eighty-one printed sketches for the costumes of five different ballets. A group of questions cannot satisfactorily be answered at present: Why are there five ballets and no operas in the series? Why do three of the productions appear within a nineteen-month period while other works from the same seasons are omitted? Why is there one "ballo" not even performed at la Scala, but rather at the Teatro Carcano? The familiar names of the Milanese publishing scene are reassuring, but Milan's only group even remotely able to satisfy amateurs of costume plates, like the Martinet series of Paris, is sketchy and poor. The aesthetic quality of the plates is almost nil. They exist simply as dance costume souvenirs (no. 387).

However, there are other Milanese series of definite merit. The Tipografia Guglielmini was responsible for three (or four) prints for the *Figaro,* a theatrical newspaper (series K). A biography of Salvatore Viganò published in 1838 included two engravings by Bertotti (series J). A group of several small books called the *Strenna Teatrale* began in 1838 with a volume that included a portrait of Domenico Ronzani costumed as a Roman warrior (series I). Cerrito, Luigia Colombon, Blasis, Grahn, Elssler, Grisi, and Ferraris appear in later volumes.

Best in quality of all the Milanese series are the illustrations contained in a series of annual almanachs of la Scala published by the Ubicini brothers beginning in 1822 (series G). The great mimes are included more often than the dancers "di rango francese." Yet Teresa Héberlé as prima ballerina in Coralli's *Statue of Venus* was in the almanach of 1826 (no. 405), as were Pallerini and Molinari seven years later (no. 417). They are shown here to convey the charm of these little colored engravings, representatives of the best of the Italian series.

The common Italian practise of spontaneous tribute to a famous star in an opera house has been previously underlined. It colors the whole of the gallery.

Nowhere else would we find a printed likeness so "like" that the sitter is unhesitatingly presented as hideous. To accompany the ugly Sofia Fuoco, what more completely unappetising partner than the young Ferdinando Walpot who appeared at the Canobbiana in the autumn of 1855 (no. 256)? Lest these monsters prejudice us too completely, remember the lovely Adelaide Frassi in the charming arabesque from Florence (no. 102). Luigia Zaccaria on one knee in an extended arabesque with Ettore Barracani hovering protectively over her (no. 257) is far more appealing than Egidio Priora sitting stiffly beside his wife Augusta Peghin (no. 177). But the Prioras, after important careers of their own, raised a daughter Olimpia who danced at the Paris Opéra as well as in Rome, Venice, Milan and Turin. If Rosina Gusman in attitude resembles Maria Tallchief like a twin (no. 122), Vincenzina Bertucci from Bologna in 1855 looks like

No. 256. Ferdinando Walpot

No. 102. Adelaide Frassi

nothing so much a provincial Italian ballerina in a city of secondary artistic importance (no. 10).

An author must be allowed favorites. Among mine are Maria Luigia Bussola watching herself in Taglioni's role from *la Figlia del Danubio* (no. 42), or Chiara Piglia as an Indian from Rome in 1832 (no. 183), or Luigia Porta dancing with a veil two years later in Turin (no. 196). Rosina Scotti at Genoa in 1854 appears in a sketchy landscape, a typical conceit of several prints of the period (no. 229). She looks strangely earthbound and "dumpy," unlike the willowy Giovannina Pitteri in Verona two years later (no. 184). And how can anyone not include the delightful character pose of the eleven-year-olds Pia Cavalieri with Ottavio Memmi (no. 153)?

A final print deserves notice. No one will remember the lovely Celestina Thierry, Adelaide Ferrari, and Puride Marra without a supplemental illustration (no. 239). This *pas de trois* by named, if not known, dancers ends our journey into the realm of equally named, if until now unknown, Italian dance prints.

No. 177. Egidio Priora and Augusta Peghin

No. 257. Luigia Zaccaria and Ettore Barracani

No. 42. Maria Luigia Bussola

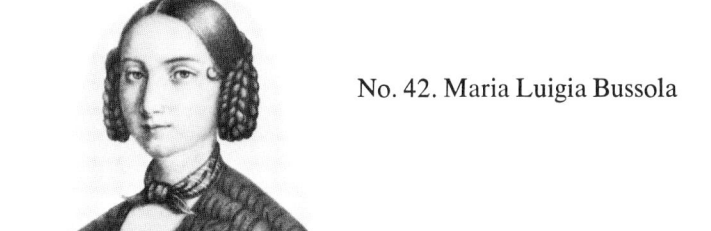

No. 122. Rosina Gusman

No. 10. Vincenzina Bertucci

No. 183. Chiara Piglia

No. 196. Luigia Porta

No. 229. Rosina Scotti

No. 184. Giovannina Pitteri

No. 153. Ottavio Memmi and Pia Cavalieri

No. 239. Celestina Thierry,
Adelaide Ferrari
and Puride Marra

INDEX TO THEATRE WORKS CITED

AGLAIJA o la FATA DEL LAGO (also IL LAGO DELLE FATE) Guerra London (Le Lac des Fées) May 14, 1840; R Oct. 30, 1843; Ve 45P **55, 454, 455**

ALESSANDRO NELL'INDIE S. Viganò S Feb. 24, 1820 **290**

Le AMAZZONI Henry Na early 1826; S Dec. 26, 1826 **409**

ANTIGONE Galzerani S June 4, 1825; Na late 1831 **406**

ARMINIO (also I CHERUSCHI) Henry Na late 1824, early 1830; S Feb. 19, 1828 **335-346, 411**

l'ASSEDIO di CALAIS (see EDOARDO III ossia l'ASSEDIO di CALAIS)

BAIAZET Galzerani S Nov. 7, 1829 **413**

BATILDE di TURENNA name given to Verdi's opera I VESPRI SICILIANI (P June 13, 1855) when first given in Na 1857 **231**

BIANCA di CASTIGLIA Morosini S Dec. 26, 1835 **422**

BIANCA di MESSINA S. Taglioni S Nov. 6, 1824 **404**

Il BUONDELMONTE Galzerani Ve Jan. 1827; Na late 1827; S Feb. 7, 1829; T (BUONDELMONTE E GLI AMEDEI) 1840-41 **76**

Il CALZOLAIO di MOMPELLIERI (also Il CIABATTINO di MONTPELLIER) S. Viganò S Oct. 16, 1819 **292**

La CAMPANELLA d'ARGENTO (also La PIANELLA d'ARGENTO) Bertini S Dec. 26, 1819 **289**

CAPRICCIO e BUON CUORE G. Gioja S Feb. 23, 1819 **293**

CATTERINA ossia la FIGLIA DEL BANDITO Perrot London Mar. 3, 1846; S Jan. 9, 1847; T 1850-51 **115**

CHAO-KANG see KAO-KANG

I CHERUSCHI (see ARMINIO)

CIMENE (also CID) S. Viganò S. Dec. 26, 1819 **291**

CLEOPATRA in TARSO Aumer S Dec. 26, 1821 **311, 315**

CRISTOFORO COLOMBO (also COLOMBO all'ISOLA di CUBA) Monticini S Nov. 3, 1832; T 1838 **418, 427**

DIRCEA Henry Mar. 27, 1826 **408**

EDOARDO III ossia l'ASSEDIO di CALAIS S Feb. 15, 1827; Na 1828 **320-334**

EMMA PRINCIPESSA del NORD ossia Il

TRIONFO d'AMORE   Horschelt   S Feb. 8, 1831 **359-377**
ESMERALDA   Perrot   London Mar. 9, 1844; S Dec. 26, 1844; Senigallia 1845; Na 1846; M (Canob.) 1849A; Ve Jan., 1850 **82, 83**
EZZELINO SOTTO le MURA di BASSANO   G. Serafini   M (Canob.) 1833C; R 1835C; T 1835-6 **207**
FAUST   S. Taglioni   Na 1838-39; Perrot S Feb. 12, 1848; T 1851-52 **237**
La FESTA di BALLO in MASCHERA   Henry   S Jan. 27, 1830; S. Taglioni T 1832 **414**
La FIGLIA del DANUBIO   F. Taglioni   P (la FILLE du DANUBE) Sept. 21, 1836; Bologna 1842A; T **42, 234**
FOLGORE o Il DEMONIO SEDUTTORE   D. Costa   Na Jan., 1861 **21**
FRANCESCA da RIMINI   Galzerani   (M Canob.) 1825A **407**
GABRIELLA di VERGY   G. Gioja   S Aug. 24, 1822; Ve Dec., 1831; Na 1837-8 **304-307**
Il GIAFFAR   G. Briol   Ve Dec., 1838; Na 1840-41; Parma 1843P **247**
GIOVANNA d'ARCO   S. Viganò   S Mar. 3, 1821; T 1825; Na early 1827 **310, 401**
La GITANA   F. Taglioni   St. Petersburg Nov., 1838; London June 6, 1839; S May 18, 1841; Bologna 1842 **232, 233**
GIULIETTA e ROMEO   F. Gioja   M (Canob.) 1833P **420**
GUGLIELMO TELL   Henry   Na 1820; S Feb. 19, 1833; T 1834 **419**
GUIDONE SELVAGGIO ossia Le GUERRIERE d'ALESSANDRA   G. Gioja   S Apr. 15, 1816 **262-275**
IDEA   P. Borri   T 1866-67 **188-190**
IMELDA e BONIFACCIO   Cortesi   S Oct. 22, 1831; T 1839 **161**
INES di CASTRO   A. Cortesi   T 1827; Ve Dec., 1829; Na 1831 P; S Sept. 4, 1831 **160, 167, 168, 417**
KAO-KANG (also CHAO KANG)   Henry   Na 1820 A; M (Carcano) 1831; P (Théâtre-Nautique) Oct. 16, 1834 **426**
KARDINUTO   Monticini   T 1842-43; S Aug. 23, †1845 **230**
Il LAGO DELLE FATE (see AGLAIJA)
MACBETH   Na A. Vestris 1818-19; Henry S Feb. 20, 1830 **443**
MARCO VISCONTI   Cortesi   S Oct. 19, 1836; Ve Mar., 1838 **423**
MARIA STUARDA   Galzerani   S Feb. 10, 1826; Ve Dec. 1826 **76**

I MINATORI di SALERNO   M (Canob.) 1837 P **424**
MIRRA osia la VENDETTA di VENERE   S. Viganò   S 1817 A **294**
La MOGLIE SAGGIA   T (?) **45**
MONSIEUR de CHALUMEAUX   Na (Fondo) 1816?; Galzerani S Jan. 14, 1834; T 1835 **442**
La MORTE d'ETTORE   Clerico   S June 2, 1821; Ve 1822-23 **402**
La MUTA di PORTICI   (Opera) P Feb. 29, 1828; S Dec. 26, 1838; Bologna; Perugia 1843 E **50**
Il NOCE di BENEVENTO   S. Viganò by G. Viganò   S Apr. 30, 1822 **316**
ORESTE   Galzerani   S. Dec. 26, 1825; Ve G. Fabris Dec., 1834 **107**
L'ORFANO di GINEVRA   M (Canob.) 1830 P **415**
Il PARIA   S. Taglioni   S Dec. 26, 1827; Na 1830-31 **410**
Il PELLEGRINO NEGROMANTE ossia La CALZOLAJA e La CONTESSA   U. Garzia   S Dec. 27, 1820 **295**
PIPELET   R (Argentina) 1861 C **12**
RENATO d'ARLES   R 1848 C **225**
Il RINNEGATO PORTOGHESE ossia GUSMANO d'ALMEIDA   M (Canob.) 1830 P; Ve (GUSMANO ...) 1837 C **416**
RITA GAUTHIER   F. Termanini   Ancona 1856 P; Ve July, 1858 **148**
ROMANOFF   S. Taglioni   S Jan. 17, 1837 **425**
I SARACENI in SICILIA   Morosini   S Aug. 16, 1834 **421**
Il SAUTING BOLL   Parma **246**
SESOSTRI   S. Taglioni   Na 1822-23; S Aug. 16, 1824 **403**
La SILFIDE   F. Taglioni   P Mar. 12, 1832; Ve Jan., 1838; T 1839, May 29, 1841; R 1843 C; Parma 1843 P; Cortesi S Jan. 27, 1841 **53, 86, 87, 432**
SOFIA di MOSCOVIA   F **164**
Il SOLITARIO   Clerico   S Feb. 16, 1825; Na (L'ORFANO di SAN MARCO o Il SOLITARIO) A. Demasier 1829-30 **308**
I SPAGNOLI nel PERU   Galzerani   S Oct. 18, 1828; Na 1830 **347-378, 412**
La STATUA di VENERE   G. Coralli   S Apr. 14, 1825 **405**
La SYLPHIDE (see La SILFIDE)
La TEMPESTA   P. Borri   T 1868-69 **467**
TIMUR KAN   P. Angiolini   S Oct. 21, 1820 **288**
La VEDOVA nel GIORNO delle NOZZE   Henry   M (Carcano) 1830-31 C **378-400**
I VENEZIANI a COSTANTINOPOLI   Monticini   Ve Jan., 1834; T 1838 **169**
La ZINGARELLA   G. Fabbri   R 1843 A **33**

bibliography

ARRIGONI, Paolo and BERTARELLI, Achille, *Ritratti di Musicisti ed Artisti di Teatro conservati nella Raccolta delle Stampe e dei Disegni* (Milano, "Popolo d'Italia," 1934) Abbrev: A/B

BEAUMONT, Cyril W. and SITWELL, Sacheverell, *The Romantic Ballet in Lithographs of the Time* (London, Faber and Faber Ltd., 1938) Abbrev: B/S

BINNEY, Edwin (3rd), *les Ballets de Théophile Gautier* (Paris, Nizet, 1965)

BINNEY, Edwin (3rd), *Royal Festivals and Romantic Ballerinas 1600-1850* (Washington, D.C., 1971)

BINNEY, Edwin (3rd), "A Century of Austro-German Dance Prints, 1790-1890," *Dance Perspectives* 47 (Autumn, 1971) Abbrev: Germ

BREGGI, Paolo, *Serie degli spettacoli rappresentati al Teatro Regio di Torino dal 1688 al presente* (Torino, 1872)

CAMBIASI, Pompeo, *la Scala, 1778-1906*, 5th edit. (Milano, G. Ricordi, [1906])

CARRIERI, Raffaele, *la Danza in Italia 1500-1900* (Milano, Editoriale Domus, 1946) Abbrev: Carr

CHAFFEE, George, "The Romantic Ballet in London 1821-1858," *Dance Index,* vol. II, nos. 9, 10, 11, 12 (Sept.-Dec., 1943) Abbrev: Eng

CHAFFEE, George, "The Romantic Ballet in London, New Mercury Ltd., 1964) Abbrev: IG, Romb tenary Salvo," *Dance Index,* vol. III, nos. 9, 10, 11 (Sept.-Nov., 1944) Abbrev: Fr

COHEN, Selma Jeanne, "Freme di Gelosia! Italian Ballet Librettos, 1766-1865," *Bulletin of the New York Public Library,* Nov., 1963 (vol. 67, no. 9)

Enciclopedia dello Spettacolo, 9 vols. (Roma, le Maschere, 1954-1962) Abbrev: E/S

FILIPPIS, F. de and ARNESE, R., *Cronache del Teatro di S. Carlo, 1737-1960,* 2 vols. (Napoli, Edizioni Politica Popolare, 1961 and 1963) Abbrev: F/A

GATTI, Carlo, *Il Teatro alla Scala nella Storia e nell'Arte (1778-1963),* 2 vols. (Milano, Ricordi, 1964)

GUEST, Ivor, *Fanny Cerrito, the Life of a Romantic Ballerina* (London, Phoenix House Ltd., 1954) Abbrev: IG, FC

GUEST, Ivor, *Fanny Elssler* (London, Adam and Charles Black, 1970) Abbrev.: IG, FE

GUEST, Ivor, *A Gallery of Romantic Ballet* (London, New Mercury Ltd., 1965) Abbrev: IG, Romb

GUEST, Ivor, *The Romantic Ballet in Paris* (London, Sir Isaac Pitman and Sons Ltd., 1954)

HALL, Lillian Arvilla, *Catalogue of Dramatic Portraits in the Theatre Collection of the Harvard College Library,* 4 vols. (Cambridge, Harvard Univ. Press, 1930-34)

KHUDYEKOV, S. H., *Istoria Tantsev,* vol. III (Petrograd, 1915) Abbrev: Kh

MIGEL, Parmenia, *The Ballerinas* (New York, Macmillan, 1972)

MOORE, Lillian, *Images of the Dance, Historical Treasures of the Dance Collection, 1581-1861* (New York, New York Public Library, 1965) Abbrev: LM

PIRCHAN, Emil, *Fanny Elssler, eine Wienerin tanzt um diet Welt* (Wien, Wilhelm Frick, 1940)

SACERDOTE, Giacomo, *Teatro Regio di Torino* (Torino, 1892)

SOLOVIEW, N. V., *Maria Taglioni* (St. Petersburg, 1912)

WINTER, Marian Hannah, "Augusta Maywood," *Dance Index,* vol. II, nos. 1-2 (Jan.-Feb., 1943) Abbrev: MHW, AM

WINTER, Marian Hannah, "Theatre of Marvels," *Dance Index,* vol. VII, nos. 1-2 (Jan.-Feb., 1948) Abbrev: MHW, DI

WINTER, Marian Hannah, *le Théâtre du Merveilleux* (Paris, Olivier Perrin, 1962) Abbrev: MHW

CATALOGUE

Part I lists the prints alphabetically according to the name of the dancer depicted. Care has been taken to make this order chronological within the listing for each performer, but the prevalence of undated prints makes an absolute chronology impossible. The series of prints are listed in Part II, alphabetically by city, then chronologically.

An asterisk before the catalogue number indicates that the print is illustrated in this issue.

In Part I, birth and death dates, where known, immediately follow the name of the dancer. Letter and date abbreviations (1800's are understood) give the known performance data of his career in Italy.

Since the major Italian opera houses gave performances during specific seasons rather than continuously throughout the year, information about these seasons is found after the year date (they should not be confused with similar letter abbreviations for the cities which precede the year dates):

C	*Carnevale*	(Carnival) The longest and most important of the seasons began at la Scala late in December of the year preceding most of its duration. Thus "40C" refers to the Carnival season which began on Dec. 26, 1839. (Other cities, whose opera houses do not list complete dates but only those of the season in which a work was first performed, are normally given dates like "40-41," "53-54," etc.)
Q	*Quaresima* (or *Quadragesima*)	(Lent) Normally Lenten seasons were combined with those of Carnival, hence "CQ." This was the period which saw the greatest of the stars at la Scala.
P	*Primavera*	(Spring) Usually a shorter season; sometimes omitted entirely.
E	*Estate*	(Summer) Seldom found at la Scala, although occasionally there was a short series of benefit performances. It is more common in the smaller cities.
A	*Autunno*	(Autumn) Occurs only occasionally, but more often than the spring seasons.

Within each catalogue entry, the following information is given:

1. Description of the print. The directions of head and body facing are those of the sitter rather than of the viewer. (In the series, the name of the dancer is given first for easier identification.)

2. Height of the printed figure, including head ornaments, in inches. If there are marginal lines or color of paper contrast, additional dimensions are given, height preceding width.

3. Names of artist, engraver or lithographer, printer, and publisher, with related data given on the print, in series separated by hyphens rather than according to exact location on the sheet. If the information is enclosed in quotation marks, it appears in printed manuscript on the original. However, if this data appears below the title of the print, it is cited after the title.

4. Title of the print if it gives more than the name of the dancer. Quotation marks indicate printed manuscript. When there are laudatory verses or other text on the print, they appear in quotation marks, prefaced by their description in parentheses: (couplet:), (tercet:), (huitain:), etc.

5. Listings of the print, if any, in published catalogues, followed by published reproductions.

6. Location of the print in private and public collections.

The "seven stalwarts," whose collections served as basis for the beginnings of this catalogue and who answered questions about their own and other holdings of Italian prints, are numbered alphabetically except for Madame de Moroda.

1. the author
2. Norman Crider, New York City
3. Allison Delarue, Princeton, New Jersey
4. Parmenia Migel Ekstrom, New York City
5. Zachary Constantine Solov, New York City
6. Marian Hannah Winter, Paris
7. F. Derra de Moroda, Salzburg

For the public repositories, the following letters refer to the specific collection as well as to the city involved:

F	Florence	
H	Harvard	and its Theatre Collection, Cambridge, Mass. Jeanne T. Newlin, curator.
L	London	and the Theatre Collection of the Victoria and Albert Museum.
M	Milan	and the collection of the Castello Sforzesco. Dottoressa Clelia Alberici, conservatrice.
N	New York	and the Dance Collection of The New York Public Library. Genevieve Oswald, curator.
Na	Naples	the theatres of the San Carlo and the Fondo as well as the branch of the Biblioteca nazionale there.
P	Paris	and the Musée et Bibliothèque de l'Opéra. Mlle. Martine Kahane, conservateur et bibliothécaire en chef.
R	Rome	the theatres Apollo (Ap.), Torre Argentina (Arg.), and Valle (Va.) with the Museo Burcardo. Dottore Cesare Branchini, conservatore.
S	la Scala	Milan and its theatrical museum. Dottore Giampiero Tintori, conservatore.
T	Turin	and the Teatro Regio.
Ve	Venice	particularly la Fenice.
Ve (Cor.)		Venice, Museo Correr and its print department. Dottoressa Lucia Bellodi-Casanova, conservatrice.
Ve (Marc.)		Venice, Biblioteca Marciana. Dottore Giorgio E. Ferrari, conservatore.

An additional note on the size of the prints: too frequently in catalogues, measurement to the edges of a sheet are given, with the notation "clipped." Inasmuch as two otherwise identical prints seldom have the same margins, and therefore have different sizes, the height of the *printed figure* has been used as sufficient guide-line. All too many past collectors mutilated their prints, clipping away parts so as to force a large sheet into a smaller scrapbook. To insist on the size of margins, when the complete figure was more usually respected, is to confuse present-day collectors who want to compare their present holdings to the prints described herewith.

To avoid pedantry and the proliferation of the notation *"sic,"* the spelling on the prints has been reproduced exactly, without further comment. Sharper eyes with more powerful magnifying glasses may take exception to some of these spellings. It is possible that they are consulting more heavily-printed examples than those used by the author.

NOTE: For simplicity, the superior letters used as abbreviations at the ends of proper names; *i.e.*, G.o for "Giorgio" or Nap.e for "Napoleone"—are reproduced with a period before the final letter or letters. This system is also used for common words like C.ia ("Compagnia"), Illustraz.e ("Illustrazione"), etc.

PART I

ANDREANOVA (ADRIANOFF), Elena (1816?-1857) S 46CQ

1 Three-quarters to slight L, head inclined R. L arm low in 2nd, R hand to L shoulder. 3⅞. Elena Andrianoff / Prima Danzatrice nell'I.R. Teatro di Pietroburgo / in costume della sua prima rappresentazione / nell'I.R. Teatro alla Scala in Milano, 1846. L. Mantovani inc. AB/105. Repr: E/S. I, 106. **MN**
Variant: with medal conferred for the occasion **M**

ARANYVARY, Emilia S 61A; Ancona 63C

2 Three-quarters to L, facing front, seated, hands crossed at waist. 8½ in rect. with rounded corners 10⅜ x 8⅜. Ad / Emilia Aránynváry / Esimia Danzatrice nel Carnevale del 1863 in Ancona. "A. Bedetti"–Lit. F.lli Pieroni, Ancona A/B 132. **MNS**

BADERNA, Marietta (b. 1830) S 46P

3 More than three-quarters to slight L, facing front, head inclined to R, hands folded below, elbows tensed. 10½. Surrounded by frame of clouds in which she appears in 16 full length poses, each about 2½. Marietta Baderna / Allieva de' Sig.ri Conjugi Blasis professori di perfezionamento all. I.R. Academia di Ballo in Milano. / Prima danzatrice all'I.R. Teatro alla Scala. / la Primavera del 1846. / Alcuni Ammiratori D. D. Giuliani dis. Lit. Messaggi Cd. del Capello 4025. Repr: LM 70. **HMNS**

BARATTI, Giovannina R 58C; S 59A, 71CQ; T 59-60, 67-68; Na 69-70

4 More than half to L, facing front, wide forehead. 6⅞. Giovannina Baratti / prima ballerina danzante nel Gran Teatro d'Apollo / in Roma il Carnevale 1858 / In segno di stima gli ammiratori D.C. D.D.D. Lit. Battistelli. A/B 225. Repr: Kh 350. **MN**
Variant: within tinted rect. 9 x 7½ **M**

BARRACANI, Ettore Ve 47 (Sept.); F 53E see 257

BEDOTTI, Antonio S 17, 18P, 20CQPA, 21P, 22CQPA, 23CQA, 24PA, 25CQ, 31CQ; M(Canobbiana) 24; Ve 31-32; Genoa 36CP

5 Bust to slight L, facing front, coat with frogs and fur collar. 6. Antonio Bedotti / Primo Ballerino mimico al Teatro Carlo Felice / in Carnevale e la Primavera del 1836. G. Isola "l'autore / all'amico Bedotti" A/B 309. **M**

BELLONI, Giuseppe S 22CQ see 315

BELLOTTI, Emma Na 56A

6 Three-quarters to front, facing front, R arm across waist low, L hand down. 8¾. Emma Bellotti / 1.a Ballerina assoluta del Teatro Nuovo / nella stagione di autunno 1856. (huitain:) "Si per la danza...." G. Giangiacomo dis.–Lit. Giusti alla Pedaccia. A/B 349. **MN**
Variant: within tinted rect. 10½ x 9¼ **M**

BENCINI (later BENCINI-MOLINARI), Giuditta see 322

BERETTA, Caterina (1839-1911) F 54A; S 56CQ, 58A, 59EA, 61CQ, 69CQ, 70CQ, 77CQ; Ancona 57P; T 57-58, 63-64, 64, 65, 70-71; Ve 58-59; Na 62-63, 65-66, 70-71 see also 458

7 Bust to slight R, facing front, crown of braids. 5¾ in tinted rect. 7½ x 6. Catterina Beretta / Prima Ballerina Danzante / Firenze, Autunno 1854. G. B. dis. A/B 389. **MN**

8 Three-quarters to R, seated. A Caterina Berretta nella Primavera del 1857 / gli Anconitani. "A. Bedetti"–Ancona, Lit. Fratelli Pieroni. A/B 413. **MS**

BERTUCCI, Vincenzina Bologna 55; Mirandola 55A; Perugia 59; R 61C

9 Full to front, head inclined L. On pointes in 5th, fingers interlaced down. 7¼. A/B 442 (proof without text). **M**

*10 Full to R, head inclined L, R foot pointe tendue croisée back, hands hold apron to front. 10¼. Vincenzina Bertucci / prima ballerina di rango francese / al Contavalli in Bologna. "A. Frulli disegnò"–Bologna Lit. Angiolini. **H**
Variant: coarser. Vincenzina Bertucci / prima ballerina di rango francese / l'Autunno del 1855 / in Mirandola. G. o Caruzzo(?) dis.–Modena Lit. Vendemiati(?) **N**

11 Full, in third arabesque on R pointes, facing R, atop a globe. 4⅝. Vincenzina Bertucci / (couplet:) "Donna gentil...!" / Fatto in Perugia in Carnevale del 1859 / per cura di alcuni ammiratori. C. Martinelli dis. **H**

12 Full to front, head inclined L, on pointes in 5th position, R forefinger to chin, L hand holds out skirt. 8¾. A Vincenzina Bertucci / Prima Ballerina assoluta / nel Teatro Argentina di Roma / nel ballo Pipelet / Carnevale 1860-1 / gli ammiratori. "V. Roscioni"–Roma, Lit. Danesi A/B 441. Repr: Kh 341, bottom R. **M**

BIANCIARDI, Carlo S 1795Q-33CQ see 274, 357

BLASIS, Annunziata (née RAMACCINI) (1818-1892) S 28CQ; R 37 see also 440

13 (companion to 16) A marble bust after Eugenio Thierry. To front, facing L. 3¾ (to bottom of socle). Gli Allievi dell'I.R. Academia / di ballo e di mimica in Milano / l'anno 1838 consacravano / ad / Annunziata Blasis. Luigi Mantovani inc. A/B 492. **M**
Variant: without name of Mantovani **NS**

BLASIS, Carlo (1799-1878) S 18CQPA, 20CQ; 22CQA, 23P; T 21, 24, 26; Ve 23-25, 31; Reggio 26 see also 431, 441, 461

14 Bust to slight L, facing front, points of high white collar beside chin. 4¾. Carlo Blasis / Primo Ballerino del Teatro del Rè / in Londra / Attuale Primo Danzatore nel Grande / Teatro la Fenice 1831. (no artists) (see also 441) A/B 494. **HMNS**
Variant: (possibly French) M. C. Blasis **1N**

15 Five busts. 2¾. Francesco Antonio de Blasis (top); Carlo de Blasis (mid L); Annunziata (mid R); Virginia (lower L); Teresa (lower R). Famiglia de Blasis. Irina-Cenzana inc. Estratto dalle Biografie de' De Blasis nell'opera *Mente e Cuore*. **S**

16 (companion to 13) A marble bust after Eugenio Thierry. To front, facing R. 4 (to bottom of socle). Text as in 13, but: Scolpsit di Eugenio Thierry–Inciso di Luigi Mantovani. (see also 431) A/B 495. Repr: Kh 209. **MN**
*Variant: whole sheet within frame of Baderna from 3. Within double rectangle 20 x 16. Giustiani dis.–Lit. Messaggi Cd. del Capello 4025. **MS**

17 More than half to slight L, facing front, seated, R elbow over chair back, hands clasped. 5½. A. Azziolidi dis.–L. Mantovani inc. A/B 498. **M**
Variant: without names of artists **MN**

BOCCI, Giuseppe S 16ff see 271, 354, 359, 402, 418

BOCCI, Maria S 16CQ-30CQ (almost every season) see 316, 348

BONALUMI, Laurina S 27PE, 28A see 351

BORRI, Pasquale (1820-1884) m. Carolina POCHINI S 40PA; 41CQPA; 42CQ; Ve 42-44, 49-51, 55-56 see also 189, 190, 467

18 Half to R, facing front, seated, L hand clenched in lap. 7¾ in tinted rect. 10¾ x 8. "DeCrescenzo dis."–Lit. Richter. **S**

BOSCHETTI, Amina (1836-1881) Na 55-56, 59-61, 64-67, 66-67, 73-74; Trieste 56; S 62CQA; Genoa 75-76 see also 459

19 Bust to rear, facing side over R shoulder, seated, hair falling down back, R elbow on chair back, R hand on chair arm. 11⅛ x 7⅞. Facs. sign. "Ferrero"–Torino, Tip Lit Camillo e Bertolero. **N**

20 Almost three-quarters to slight R, facing front, braids around hair, R hand on trellis (?); in landscape. 7¾. Amina Boschetti / in Trieste nel 1856. "V. Poiret"–Lit. B. Linassi. **S**

*21 with three others. Whole group 8 x 6 in rect. with rounded corners 11¾ x 10½. "Passo a Quattro / eseguito da' primi Ballerini assoluti Sig.a Amina Boschetti e Sig.r Dario Fissi / in unione dell'altra Ballerina Sig.a Giuseppina De Rosa, e del Mimo Amoroso Sig.r Nicola Fusco /

nel Ballo FOLGORE dato al Real Teatro S. Carlo nel Gennajo 1861. / Composto e Diretto dal Coreografo Sig.r Davide Costa" Filippo del Buono Figurista de' Reali Teatri dipinse... **H**

*22 Almost three-quarters to front, facing front, head inclined slightly down, both hands hold out complicated peplum. 9. Facs. sign. "DeCrescenzo fec."–Lit. Frat. Perrotta. **N**

23 Half to extreme L, facing half L over R shoulder, in costume with beads. 7¼. Amina Boschetti. 1863 A/B 606. **M**

24 Three-quarters to R, facing front, seated. 7. Lit. Gius. Hennert al Largo Montecalvario. A/B 607. Repr: F/A II, 251. **M**
Variant: same. Marta dis.–Lit. Gatti e Dura **S**

25 Bust to full L, facing almost front over R shoulder, long earrings, jewels in hair and hanging. 7 in octagon 9½ x 6. Galleria del Nuovo Trovatore / Amina Boschetti / Nell'Arte della Danza Celebre...Lit. L. Rossetti C.D.P. **S**

26 Celebrità Danzanta al Carlo Felice di Genova / Stagione 1875-76. 9½ x 6½ (size of complete sheet). Lit. Armanino. **4**

BOSE, Enrichetta S 68 (winter); 74CQ, T 74-75

27 Bust to half R, facing full R, flowers behind ear and over L shoulder. 10⅛ in oval 12 x 9⅜. F. Vinea dis. A/B 608. **MS**

28 Bust to slight L, facing slight R, frizzy hair, lockets. 4¾. (no artists) **S**

29 (possibly not an Italian print) Three-quarters to slight R, facing front, R elbow on chair back, L arm down, long black dress. 13 in tinted rect. 17½ x 12½. Henriette Boce. M. Krantz lith. **S**

BRESSAC, Pauline S 54CQ; Rovigo 55A

30 Bust to slight R, facing front. 6½. Paolina Bressac / Prima Ballerina Assoluta di rango francese / Teatro di Rovigo, autunno 1855. (no artists) (five verses:) "Addio bella e gentil..." A/B 681. **M**

BRETIN, Luigi m. Flora FABBRI S 38CQPA; 40A; T 39, 44-45; Ve 39-40, 47 (Sept.); R (Ap.) 43C, (Alibert) 43A; Parma 43P

31 Long bust to front, facing front, black tie. Luigi Bretin / Primo Ballerino Assoluto / al Gran Teatro d'Apollo in Roma nel Carnevale 1843 / D.C.D.D.D. "V. Battistelli dis."–Lit. Battistelli. A/B 684. **14HMNS**

32 (with Flora Fabbri) Two half lengths. Fabbri: in costume, to slight L, facing front. 4. He: to slight L, facing L, suit coat, arms crossed. 3⅝. Copia Bretin / In Parma la Primavera del 1843. Bacchini dis.–Lit. Vigotti e C. A/B 865, 1466. **MN**

*33 (with Fabbri) He (L side): full to front, facing L, weight on L, offering her a flower in L hand. 10⅛. She: full to slight R, facing front, in attitude croisée back, on R pointes, R forearm behind back, L arm low in 2nd. 8½. Luigi Bretin Flora Fabbri-Bretin / primi Ballerini assoluti nel nobile Teatro Alibert nel ballo "La Zingarella" composto dal coreografo Giovanni Fabbri / Roma, l'autunno del 1843. V. Battistelli dis.–Lit. Battistelli. A/B 686, 1466. Repr: Kh 343; E/S IV, 1747. **HM**

BRUGNOLI, Amalia (b. pre-1810) m. Paolo SAMENGO Ve 20-21, 36-38; Na 23-28, 33-35; S 26P, 29PA, 30CQ; Faenza 37 (June); F 37A; R 40P see also 296, 445, 466

34 Almost three-quarters to slight L, facing front, hat with two feathers; long, filmy sleeves, pendant with three pearls at cleavage. 8 in rect. 9¾ x 8¼. Amalia Brugnoli-Samengo / Venezia 1837 Eug. Pianta dis.–Lit. Barozzi. A/B 709. **4MS**

35 Bust, with 4 others. To slight L, facing slight L, ribbons behind braided bun. 4. Artisti / In Faenza nel Giugno 1837 / 1. Giuseppina Strepponi 2. Amalia Brugnoli-Samengo / 3. Napoleone Moriani / 4. Domenico Cosselli 5. Felice Varese. G. Mattioli fece–Forli Lit. M.R. A/B 713, 1100, 3000, 4257, 4559. **M**

36 Full to R, facing L over L shoulder [illegible] Matthis who supports her from behind. 1⅝. In scene with cottage to L. 3 x 6. MUSIC COVER. Pas Styrien eseguito della Sig.a Brugnoli e Sig. Matthis / nella stagione autunnale del 1837 / all' I.e R. Teatro di via della Pergola / Florence chez Joseph Lorenzi et Fils dans la Place St. Laurent. **1**

*37 Full to L, facing front, R foot pointe tendue front, both hands on shoulders. 10¼. Amalia Brugnoli Samengo / Prima Ballerina Danzante nel Gran Teatro d'Apollo / in Roma la Primavera del 1840. Lit. Martelli. A/B 710. **MN**

38 Half to slight R, facing almost front, flowers as a tiara extending to ears, print dress with stripes. 6. Amalia Brugnoli-Samengo / Prima ballerina nella Primavera 1840. Pietro Bindi dis. dal vero. A/B 711. **M**

BUSSOLA, Maria Luigia S 41CQP, 42CQPA; Verona 45C; Reggio 46; Brescia 47; R 51A; Asti 55A; T

39 A poem of 5 quatrains: "Sei fatta d'aere..." in ornamental frame with garland pas de deux above. 3; pas de trois below. 2½. Single figures on sides. Whole: 13½ x 9¼. A / Maria Luigia Bussola / nel Carnevale / 1844-45 / in Verona. F. Penuti fec.–Lit. Guelmi. **S**

40 Half to slight R, facing front, arms down. 7½. Luigia Bussola / Prima Ballerina assoluta / nel Teatro di Reggio la Fiera dell'Anno 1846. (no artist) A/B 734. **M**

41 Almost three-quarters to slight R, facing front, seated, rose at center of cleavage. 7⅞. (names in wreath). Brescia Lit. Filippini–"A. Ogheriy" (for Oghieri) / 1847: / (tercet:) "Bella e gentile...." **M**

*42 Above: three-quarters to R, facing slight R, braids in curls over ears, hands crossed in lap. 7¾. Below: First arabesque on R, facing L. 2½. Maria Luigia Bussola / nel ballo la Figlia del Danubio. / (quatrain:) "Ah le tue caste danze...." Janelli F.co dis.e lit.–Torino, Lit. Doyen e C.ia. A/B 736. **M**

43 Full to front, head inclined R, 5th position on pointes, R forefinger to chin, L arm low to side. 8⅞. Luigia Maria Bussola / Roma, l'Autunno 1851. A/B 735. **1HMNS**

CANTELLI, Emilia Bologna 55C

44 Half to L, facing front, shirred edge on top and bottom of bodice. 4⅞ in tinted rect. 6⅛ x 5⅛. Emilia Cantelli / Danzatrice al Teatro Contavalli di Bologna / gli Ammiratori nel Carnevale 1855 / D.D.D. Minardi dis.–Lit. Angiolini. **1**

CASATI, Giovanni S 27CQ, 28CQPA, 29CQPA, 31CQ see 324, 356, 361, 364

CATENA, Adelaide S 41CQP, 42 CQP

45 Three-quarters to slight R, facing almost front, L hand across waist with fan, R hand on top of column. 10½ in tinted rect. 12¾ x 10½. Adelaide Catena / nel Balletto La Moglie saggia. Janelli dis. dal vero–Torino, Lit. Doyen e C., 1844 A/B 859. **M**

CATTE, Effizio T 25; S 26PA, 27PE, 38-63, 68 (winter), 69CQ, 70CQ; Ve 27-29 see 427

CAVALIERI, Pia R 55P see 153

CERRITO, Fanny (1817-1907) Na 32-35; R 33C, 43A, 45C; F 33A, 34C, 44 (Feb.), 45 (Nov.); T 35A, 36C, 46CQ; S 38PA, 39CQP, 40CQ, 41CQ, 43CQ; Trieste 38C; Vicenza 38E, 39E; Brescia 38E, 39E; Padua 39E; Cremona 39E; Bergamo 40A; Verona 40A, 44 (Nov.); Perugia 43E; Parma 44 (Jan.) see also 429, 438, 454, 455

46 (related to 101) Half to front, facing directly R, hair in front of ear, jewel at cleavage. 4¼. Madame Fany Cerrito. V. Nesti inc. A/B 904. Repr: IG, FC, Ia. **MN**

47 Three-quarters to slight R, facing front, seated, rose over L ear, both hands in lap. 13½. Teresa Rondelli–Lit. Vassalli. Repr: IG, FC, Xb. **7N**

48 Half to slight R, facing front, scarf around upper arms, black dress. 8. "Ciabatti" Lit. Ballagny (A Florentine print). **S**

49 Third arabesque on R pointes, arms rounded, facing front. (no titling). (sestet:) "Dico al Pittor...." Battaglia dis. dal vero–Torino, Lit. Michele Ajello e Doyen, 1835. A/B 883. Repr: F/A II, 211; IG, FC, Ib. **MS**

*50 Half to L, facing front, roses at cleavage and on R side of hair. 6. Fanny Cerrito / (tercet:) *Muta, incesti.... / *Sostenne mirabilmente la parte di Fenella nello Spartito La Muta di Portici di Auber sul Regio Teatro della Scala. "Frulli dis.–Lit. Zannoli" A/B 885. **1HM**
Variant A: titled for Bologna; same poem; same artists; N (in tinted rect. 7⅞ x 6), S (in tinted rect. 7½ x 6) **4NS**
Variant B: (new poem). "Vano rimani l'encomio / Ove il Tuo Nome è scultro" / in Perugia / L'Estate 1843. In tinted rect. 7¼ x 6. Repr: Kh 266 middle. **M**
Variant C: (same, but no poem). 5⅞. G. Bacchini lit. Parma–Lit. Vigotti e C. A/B 896 **M**

*51 Dedication within ornamental frame. Pas de deux above; pas de trois below; single figures, with castanets on L, with closed fan on R. Whole: 9½. A / Fanny Cerrito / Mirabile / per la Grazia delle danze / e della persona / M.C.N.M. / Vicenza MDCCCXXXIX (no artists). **S**

52 Wreath: A / Fanny Cerrito / Brescia 1839. (no figure of the dancer). A hanging cloth held by two flying angels. (poem:) "Tu scendi in uman velo..." Whole: 15. G. Motta dis.—Brescia Lit. Filippini. **S**

53 Arabesque sautée on R, to slight R, facing slight L, arms down holding nest of birds. 14½. Fanny Cerrito / nel ballo la Silfide di Cortesi / Al Signor Bartolomeo Merelli che diede occasione ai Milanesi / di ammirare sulle scene del Gran Teatro della Scala / l'Esimia Artista / l'autore Roberto Focosi D.D.D. "Focosi"—Milano, Lit. Gallina. Repr: IG, FC, IIIa; LM, 63. **NS**

54 Full to L, kneeling on L knee, looking up at a falling rose. Fanny Cerrito / (tercet:) "La grazie tutte dell'Acheo..." / Roma / nell'Autunno del 1843 (no artists) A/B 886. **MS**

*55 Full to front, facing front, floating in air under huge ballooning cloak (reverse of Eng. 20; B/S 55, pl. 39 without supplementary floating figures). 6½ in scalloped frame 10 x 8¼. Fanny Cerrito / Nel Ballo Fantastico / Aglaja o la Fata del Lago / Roma nell'Autunno 1843 / D.C.D.D.D. (no artists) A/B 887. Repr: Kh 336. **1MS**
Variant A: same but without frame and D.C.D.D.D. **MN**
Variant B: same as MUSIC COVER Souvenirs / de / Fanny Cerrito / Trois airs de danse pour le Piano-Forte / ...dansé par / M.11 Cerrito / pendant l'Automne de l'année 1843 / à Rome. A/B 888. **MN**
(for additional variants see 454 and 455)

56 Full to R front, facing L, jumping in arabesque; R arm up, L arm across waist, feet badly pointed. G.F. disegnò—Bologna Lit. Cipriani. **COLOGNE**

57 More than three-quarters to front, facing front, head inclined slight R, Cupid with crown under outstretched L arm. 10¼ in rect. 11½ x 9¼. Fanny Cerrito / nel Gran Teatro di Apollo in Roma / Carnevale del 1845. V. Battistelli dis.—N. Carta dip.—Lit. Battistelli. A/B 890; Hall 32. Repr: Kh 336. **HM**

58 Three-quarters to front, facing front, L hand at bosom. 8¼ in double rect. 11 x 8½. (from Fr. 549—Ondine from *les Beautés de l'Opéra*). All'Esimia Danzatrice / Fanny Cerrito Saint Léon / nel Carnevale dell'anno 1845-46 / nel Regio Teatro di Torino. Lit.o Junck. A/B 891. **MS**

59 Three-quarters to slight L, facing front, head inclined R, R hand down holds one end of scarf, L hand under R elbow. 12 in double octagon 14 x 11¼. Facs. sign. E. Kaulbach dip.—L.G. dis.—Roma Lit. Martelli. A/B 894; Repr: Kh 266 bottom. **MNP**

60 Three-quarters to front, facing front, hands flat down, in costume, probably as Esmeralda. 10. Mad.lla Fanny Cerrito. "Masutti"—Lit. Kier. in Venezia. A/B 895. **MVe (Cor.)**

CHIARINI, Virginia and Flora (rope dancers)

61 Virginia: first arabesque on L, with garland displayed behind her back. Flora: first arabesque on R, with flag in R and wreath in L. Virginia Chiarini. Flora Chiarini / la sera del 21 N.bre 1831. nel Teatro degli Intrepidi in Firenze. (two quatrains) "D. Gaglier" A/B 949. Repr: MHW 100. **M**

62 Flora: attitude croisée back on L, head inclined L, L hand front, on shoulder of Virginia who supports her. 5¾ in oval 7⅜ x 6⅛. (without titling) A/B 950. Repr: MHW 101. **M**
NOTE: It is probable that this print was miscatalogued at the time of the publication of A/B. It is without titling. However, the identical print, with titling, exists: Teresa Monticini / (quatrain:) "Grazie, che meste nel mirar la Diva..." Giuseppe Cesari pin e del—Gio. Antonio Zuliani inc.—Pubblietto in Trieste da Giuseppe Sardi e Comp. lito. giu.o 1803. **N**

CHIOCCHIA, Odoardo S 19P, 20CQ, 21CQA; Ve 26-27; Genoa 32

63 Bust to slight L, facing front, L hand in buttoned coat. 8¼. Odoardo Chiocchia / Primo Ballerino del Teatro Italiano. L. Martini dis. 1832—Litog. Ponthenier. (A Genoese print). **M**

CIOTTI, Filippo S 16P-25CQ (almost without interruption) see 273

CLERICI, Rosa T 40, 40-41, 45A; Ve 42-43

64 Full to R, facing up to front, in third arabesque on R, wreath up in R hand. 14¼ in octagon 17 x 14½. Rosa Clerici / (Torino l'Autunno del 1845). F. Seghesio dis. dal vero e lit.—Con permiso 1845—Torino Lit. Doyen e C.ia. A/B 993. **M**

COLOMBON, Luigia m. Giovanni BRIOL S 35A, 37A, 38CQ; Na 40-44, 46-50 see also 430

65 Three-quarters to slight R, facing front, seated, rose in L hand down. 6¾. Facs. sign. F. Kaiser dis. **MS**

66 More than half to slight L, facing front. L hand on bosom, R arm down, holding scarf. 8. Luigia Colombon-Briol. L. DeCrescenzo dis.—litog. Wenzel. **M**

67 Half to slight R, head inclined L. R hand on L wrist, L elbow supported on cushion. 7 in rect. 8¾ x 6¾. Luisa Colombon-Briol / Prima Mima de' Reali Teatri in Napoli. (two quatrains) Lit. Paci. **1**

CONTI, Marietta (or Maria) S05P, 08Q, 09P, 10P, 18A, 19CQ, 20P, 25P, 27CQA, 28CQA, 29CQA, 30CQ, 33CQ, 34CQ; T 06, 08; Na 17-18, 24-25; Ve 25-26 see 276, 297, 328, 351, 409, 410, 412, 414, 419

COPPINI, Cesare Perugia 43; Ve 44-45, 58-59, 66-67; R 58A, 61; T 65-67, 69-70, 71; Genoa 73C; S 81ff

68 Long bust to R, facing front, wide bow tie, chain hanging under coat. 6⅝. Cesare Coppini / Primo Ballerino Assoluto / in Roma nel Teatro Argentina Autunno 1858. dis. Battistelli e lit. Corso 145. A/B 1057. **HMN**

CORALLI, Giovanni (1779-1854) S 09CQPA, 10C, 11C, 12CQ, 14CQ, 16CQ, 20A; Bologna 13; Ve 19 see also 277

*69 (with his wife Teresa) Two medals with profile heads and both names. He (above) to L; she (below) to R. Each: 3 in rondel 3¼. "C. Capuri f." A/B 1063, 1068. **HMS**

70 (companion to 71) Bust to front, facing L, points of high collar beside chin. 5⅞ in oval 6¼ x 5. Giovanni Coralli / Primo Ballerino al R. Teatro della Scala / al servizio di S.M. il Re d'Italia. Fran.co Scotto dis.—Luigi Rados inc.—Milano presso Ferd.o Artaria dicontro al Regio Teatro alla Scala. A/B 1065. Repr: E/S III, 1422. **47MS**

CORALLI, Teresa S 09CQPA, 10C, 11CQ, 12CQ, 14CQPA, 23CQ; Bologna 13; Ve 14-15 see also 278

71 (companion to 70) Bust to R, facing front, head inclined L, cameo in center of three-strand headband. 5½ in oval 6¼ x 5. Teresa Coralli / Prima Ballerina (remainder as in 70) A/B 1066. **157HMNS**

CORTESI, Antonio (1796-1879) T 26, 27, 28, 29, 34; Ve 29-30, 32-33, 35-36, 37-38; Genoa 36; S 27-45 see 463

COSTA, Luigi S 09CQ, 11A, 12CQPA, 13PEA, 14A, 17PA, 18A, 19CQ, 27A, 28CQP see 279

CUCCHI, Claudina (1838-1913) M (Canobbiana) 51C; S 54CQ, 64CQ; Na 71-73; T 74-75

72 Three-quarters to L, facing front, R forefingers on chair, L hand under R elbow, fringed shawl. 10¾. Claudina Cucchi / assoluta prima ballerina danzante / All I.R. Teatro della Cannobbiana / nel Carnevale del 1850-51. Milano, Stabili Saldini. **S**

73 (reverse of Germ. 45, dated 1858) Three-quarters to full R, facing front, rose in R hand down over L. 6 in rect. 7 x 5. Virginio dis.—Litog. Junck, Torino. A/B 1146 (with biography pp. 145-49 by Pompeo della Riva). **M**
Variant: without name of Virginio, nor the biography **H**

74 Three-quarters to slight R, facing further R, in costume with hanging tassels. 6¼. In rocky landscape surrounded by oval of leaves with names of ballets. 12¼ x 11 (no titling except her name). **S**

75 Three-quarters to front, facing R, seated, head balanced on L hand, L elbow on arm of chair. 9½. (fr. newspaper *Cosmorama Pittoresco*). **S**

DeMARTINI, Luigia Ve 21-22, 26-27; S 28P

76 Bust to slight L, facing slight R, finger curls across forehead. 2⅞. Luigia Demartini / (couplet:) "Riso, pianto, dolor..." / Nel Carnevale 1827 al Gran Teatro la Fenice / pei due balli, Maria Stuarda e Buondelmonte. V. Dal Favero dis.—R. Annibale inc. A/B 1233. **1MNSVe(Cor.)**

77 Half to full L, facing almost front, rose shown above R ear. 3⅝. Luigia Demartini / (couplet:) "Nell'agil piede..." P. Berolfadi dip.—G. Asioli inc. A/B 1234. **MS**

78 Bust to slight R, facing front, scarf buttoned on L shoulder, no hair showing. 4½. (no artists). **M**

De PAOLIS, Teresa F 22; Ve 32-33

79 Bust to slight L, facing front. Trident earring on R ear, coronet of braids. 3. (no artists) A/B 3245. **M**

DeROSA, Giuseppina see 21

DeVECCHI, Carolina S 31CQ, 38A see 363

DIANI, Prospero M(Canobbiana) 60C see 107

DUPAIN, Antoinette S 16CQ, 21PA see also 280

80 Half to slight R, facing R, tiara with pearl in front of fan of hair. 6. Antonia Dupen. Boucheron inc. A/B 1377. **MS**

DURAND, Eugenio Ve 52-53; Na c.57; S 60CQ see 231

ELSSLER, Fanny (1810-1884) Na 25-28, 46; S 38CQ, 44CQ, 45CQ, 47CQ, 48CQ; R 45A, 46C, 46A; Ve 45-46; Senigallia, Bologna, Ancona 45; Cesena, Foligno 46; F 47 see also 435, 450

81 Half to L, facing L, lace edging on squared collar. 9¾ in tinted rect. 11¼ x 9½. Gemelli lit.–Torino, Doyen e C., 1844. A/B 1437. **M**

82 Full to front, facing R, arabesque croisée on R pointes, L hand behind hip, R hand up, neck height; the kneeling Gringoire on L; Djali the goat on R; houses and cathedral behind. She: 4⅞. MUSIC COVER. Esmeralda Walzer / per Piano-Forte / di G. Tutsel / dall'Editore dedicati alla celebre danzatrice M.lla Fanny Elssler. Sommariva dis. Milano–Lit. Corbetta. A/B 1447. Repr: E/S IV, tav. CLXV (opp. p. 1423). **M**

*83 (same pose as 82) (no scene). 4⅞. Fanny Elssler / in Senigallia 1845 / Lito. Gionantonj. **N**

84 (after the Kriehuber portrait of 1845; Germ. 70) Half to front, facing L, L elbow on cushion, inset across plunging "V" of neckline. 5¾ in tinted rect. 6⅞ x 5¾. Fanny Elssler / Roma l'Autunno 1845. P.G. lit.–Roma, Lit. Danesi. A/B 1438. **MNS**
*Variant A: "Frulli dis."—Bologna, Lit. Angiolini. A/B 1443 **15M**
Variant B: Monti dis.–Ancona, Lit. Gianantonio **MUNICH**
Variant C: Fanny Elssler / Roma nel Carnevale del 1846 (no artists) A/B 1440 **15MN**
Variant D: Fanny Elssler / Roma nell'Autunno del 1846. Lit. Battistelli. A/B 1441 **MN**
Variant E. (reversed) Fanny Elssler / Roma nel Carnevale del 1846. V. Roscioni dis.–Roma, Lit. Martelli. A/B 1442 **1MN**
(also occurs without name of Martelli)

85 Three-quarters to full R, facing front, flowers down in L hand, R hand on waist. 7 in tinted rect. 8¼ x 6. Fanny Elssler / Cesena 1846. "Frulli dis."–Bologna Lit. Angiolini. A/B 1444. **M**

FABBRI, Flora m. Luigi BRETIN S 38A; R 43CQ, 43A; Parma 43P; T 44-45, 48-49 see also 32, 33

*86 Full to slight R, facing front, first arabesque sautée on R. 13¼. Flora Fabbri-Bretin / nell'applauditissimo ballo la Silfide / (huitain:) "Giovinetta, al pie leggero..." / Nel Gran Teatro d'Apollo in Roma Carnevale 1843 / In Segno di Stima gli ammiratori D.to C.ra DDD. "V. Battistelli dis.–Lit. Battistelli". A/B 1464. **1HMNS**

87 (same pose; smaller, reversed) 6½. Flora Fabbri-Bretin / nel Ducale Teatro di Parma / Primavera 1843. Augusto Baritz(?) dis. A/B 1463. (from this print, a French one was designed by V. Coindre). **67MN**

FARINA-REGA, Francesca Na; Bologna 30; S 33A

88 (with Nicola Marchese) Two busts, to front, she facing slight L; he facing slight R. Each: 5¼. Fr.ca Farina Rega Nicola Marchesi / Primi Ballerini della R. Accademia e Teatri di Napoli / Alcuni ammiratori in Bologna l'anno 1830. D.D.D. F. Belvedere Fece.–Lit. Cipriani e C. A/B 1496, 2575. **M**

FERRARI, Adelaide M (Canobbiana) 47C; S 49CQ see 239

FERRARIS, Amalia (1830-1904) S 41P, 42CQ, 44A, 68 (winter); Genoa 49C; T 49-50, 52-53; Na 50-52, 68-69; F 53; Vicenza 53; R 54C, 56C; Ve 54-55; Bologna 57 (winter) see also 433

89 Full to slight L, facing front under upraised R arm, attitude sautée on R, L hand behind waist, reflected in mirror behind; interior scene. 8½ in rect. with rounded corners 13¾ x 9. Amalia Ferraris / Prima Ballerina Francese / Danzava al Teatro Carlo Felice in Genova il Carnevale 1848-49. Genova, Lit. L. Doyen e C. A/B 1555; B/S 68. Repr: A/B Tav. VI (opp. p. 112); B/S 49. **M**

90 More than half to slight L, facing front, hands crossed in front of waist, locket holds tie at neck. 7¼. Facs. sign. DeCrescenzo dip. **5MNS**

91 Full to very slight R, facing front, head inclined slight L, attitude croisée on L pointes, both arms in high 5th. 13⅛. Amalia Ferraris / Vicenza 1853. B. Marcovich fect.–Vicenza Lit. Longo. Repr: LM 72. **2N**

92 Three-quarters to slight R, facing front, seated, tambourine in lap under crossed hands. 9½ in double rect. 11¾ x 9¼. Facs. sign. / Roma Carnevale 1854 / D.C.D.D.D. Battistelli dis. e Lit. A/B 1556. Repr: Kh 290, bottom L. **1245HMN**

93 Three-quarters to slight L, facing front, R hand holds closed fan across L arm which is down. Amalia Ferraris / Prima Ballerina Assoluta / nel Teatro d'Apollo il Carnevale 1856 / D.C.D.D.D. V. Battistelli dis. e lit. A/B 1557. Repr: Kh 285 R. **15HMN**

94 Third arabesque on R pointes, facing front, hands amplified up. 8¾. Completely clipped from its sheet so that nothing remains but the figure. (Probably Italian.) **2**

95 Full to L, facing front, 5th position on pointes, hands clasped in front of neck. 8½ in tinted rect. 9¾ x 9¼. MUSIC COVER. Al Genio della Danza / Amalia Ferraris / Polka Brillante / sopra motivi dell'Aroldo del Cav. Verdi / composta da.... Alessandro Magotti / Op. 12. A. Frulli dis.–Lit. Borgo Salamo. A/B 1560. Repr: F/A II, 239. **M**

FIORETTI, Angelina (1846-1879) S 61CQ, 73CQ, 75CQ

96 Full to front, facing front, R foot pointed across L, chin in R hand, L hand across waist, supports R elbow. 9½. V. Cassettaro–Lit. Antonelli (probably Venetian). **N**

FISSI, Dario Na 61 see 21

FITZ-JAMES, Nathalie (b. 1819) T 42-44, 47-48; F and Genoa 44; S 44A; Trieste 46CQ; Na 48-50 see also 456

97 Full to R, facing R, in first arabesque on R pointes, R arm rounded. 5½. A / Natalia Fitz James / Nel Carnevale-Quadrigesima / 1845-46 / (sonnet:) "Come il vento..." / Teatro Grande di Trieste. (no artists) **S**

98 Half to front, facing R, L elbow on column, hands clasped. 7½. L. DeCrescenzo dis.–Litog. Wenzel. Repr: Kh 143 top. **M**

FRASSI, Adelaide S 31CQA, 33CQA, 35CQ, 37CQ, 38CQ; R43A; Leghorn 51C

99 Half to slight R, facing front, severe black dress, arms down. 8¾. Adelaide Frassi / Prima Ballerina nel Teatro Argentina / Roma Autunno 1843. V. Battistelli dis.–Lit. Battistelli. A/B 1637. **1M**

100 Half to slight L, facing front, head inclined R, arms down, 8 pearls on pins in hair. 6½. (couplet:) "Beati gli occhi..." Domenichini dis.–Lit. Guitti (probably Ferrarese). **S**

101 (related to 46) Half to front, head inclined L, roses at cleavage and over R ear. 4¼. V. Nesti inc. A/B 1639. **M**

*102 Full to L, facing front, arabesque on L pointes, arms front. 6 in double rect. 10⅛ x 7¾. Adelaide (roses) Frassi. "Gaglier"–Lit. Ballagny. A/B 1638. **4HMN**

Variant: (roses between names) / il Carnevale del 1850 in 1851 / a Livorno. Litografia Mazzinghi Via. Sr. Francesco, N.27, Livorno. **N**

FRASSI, Carolina S 32A

103 Full to front, facing L, long dress with train, plumes in hat, arms outstretched. 14. Carolina Frassi / (quatrain:) "Nè suon di lira...." / Battistelli dis. dal vero–Con permissione 1835–Torino, Lit. di M.le Ajello e Doyen. A/B 1630. **M**

FUOCO, Sofia (1830-1916) S 43 (July), 53CQ; Ve 51-52, 53-54; R 52A, 55C; Modena 53P; Faenza 55E; Perugia 56; Trieste 57 (Feb.)

104 Half to slight R, facing front, eyes R, shirred white inset to waist. 7½. Sofia Fuoco / Teatro Argentina l'Autunno 1852. Roma, Lit. Battistelli. A/B 1681. **MN**

*105 Almost three-quarters to slight L, facing front, heart shape of head accentuated by two "peaks" of hair. 7½. Sofia Fuoco / I Modensi / La Primavera 1853. "Zattara dis."–Lit. Goldoni. A/B 1682. **1HMNS**
Variant:... / I Faentini / nell'estate dell'anno 1855 **S**

106 Full to R, facing front, head inclined R, hands holding front of skirt, weight on L, R foot pointe tendue croisée front. 7¼ in floral oval 11¼ x 8¾. Sofia Fuoco / nella / Tarentella. "Danesi"–Lit. Ach. Paris, Firenze. A/B 1683. Repr: Carr 56; LM 74; E/S V, 770. **HMNS**

FUSCO, Nicola Na 61 see 21

GAGLIANI (or GALLIANI), Carlo Ve 23-24, 25-26, 33-35; S 31CQ see also 362, 365-67, 375

107 Five busts about 4½ x 6. (Top) Gagliani Carlo Pezzoli Francesca (center) Diani Prospero (bottom) Scannagatti Carolina Rossi Giacomo / Primi Ballerini Mimici / Nel Nobil Teatro di Apollo / nel Carnevale

1838 / Nel gran Ballo Oreste, composto e / diretto dal Coregrafo Giovanni Fabris. (no artists). A/B 1270, 1718, 3416, 3828, 4072.
13HMN

GALLETTI, Carolina (1826-1905) m. Francesco ROSATI T 40-41, 41-42, 53-54; R 41C, 42C; S 45A, 46A; Na 55-56

108 Half to R, facing L, hanging braids held together. 6¼. Carolina Galletti / (quatrain:) "Move leggiadra e mille…" "Gandolf" lit. Torino–con permis. 1838–Lit. Doyen e C. A/B 1729. **M**

*109 Full to slight R, facing front, head inclined L, R foot pointe tendue in 2nd, hands behind waist. 9. Al merito della Prima Ballerina Danzante / Carolina Galletti / nel nobile / Teatro di Apollo in Roma Carnevale 1841. (no artists) A/B 1730. Repr: F/A II, 227. **1MNS**
Variant: same, but 1842. A/B 1730

110 Full to front, facing L, 5th position on pointes, R arm behind waist, L arm down. 7¾ in rect. with rounded corners 8¼ x 5¾. Carolina Rosati / (Polka di Corsaro). (no artists) **N**

GAMBARDELLA, Teresa F 44E; later with troupe of Maywood

111 Full to R, facing front over L shoulder, in Spanish costume, castanets, R arm up, L across waist, R foot pointe tendue croisée back. 6¾. Teresa Gambardella / Prima Ballerina Assoluta nell'I.e.R. Teatro degli / Intrepidi l'Estate del 1844, in Firenze. / (tercet:) "Come penna leggiera…" D. Gaglier dis.–Lit. Ridolfi. Repr: MHW, AM, p. 11. **S**

GIOJA, Ferdinando Na 1791C ff-07; S 07CQ, 10C; T 11, 15 see 112

GIOJA, Gaetano (1768-1826) S 1791C, 84CQ, 95C, 07CQ, 10C; Na 1795ff; Bologna 13, 16, 17; F 20 see also 281, 298, 448

*112 (with his brother Ferdinando) Two busts in rondels; cupid above, tambourine on edge between; names in border of rondels. 2½ (diam.) A. Volpini dis.–Lassinio inc. **H**

113 Bust to R, facing slight R, high stock and collar. 3¾ in circle 4½. Gaetano Gioja / Compositore, e Direttore di Balli. (no artists) prob. c. 1800. **1N**

114 Bust to R, facing almost front. 3½. Below: Tambourine, wands, mask, and names of his ballets. Gaetano Gioja / Insigni Choreographo / Florentina Lactatur / 1820. Lasinio Figlio inc. **S**

GOLDONI, Giovanni S 13P, 21CQ, 22A, 25P, 26CQP, 27PEA, 28PA, 29A, 37A, 44CQ see 355

GRAHN, Lucile (1819-1907) S 44CQ; Ve 46-47 see also 432

115 (from Brandard's print as Catarina, Eng. 71) Full to front, musket in hand. 11 in rect. 15½ x 11. Lucilla Grahn. V. Battistelli dis.–Roma, lit. P. Battistelli. A/B 1947. **M**

GRANZINI (or GRANCINI), Carolina S (pupil) 38ff, 41P; Ve 46 (Apr.)

116 Three-quarters to slight R, facing front, arms extended to R, palms down, frizzy curls over ears. A / Carolina Granzini / la Presidenza del Teatro Eretenio / offeriva / nell'estate del 1844. B. Marcovich dis.– Venezia, pr. lit. Kier. **H**

GRASSI, Adelaide S (pupil) 18ff, 19P, 23PA, 24CQPA; Ve 29-30; R 32C see also 288

117 Long bust to slight L, facing almost front, high "fan" of hair in coronet of braids. Ferronière. 9. Adelaide Grassi / Prima Ballerina assoluta / nel Nobile Teatro di Apollo nel Carnevale del 1832 / (five verses:) "O ha chi ti stima.…". "F. Garzoli dis.–Lit. Battistelli." **1N**

118 (with Egidio Priora) Two busts in costume, turned to face slightly toward each other. She with separate "fans" of hair. Each: 7¼. Adelaide Grassi Egidio Priora / Primi Ballerini assoluti / nel Nobil Teatro di Apollo nel Carnevale del 1832. "Almerini dis.–Roma, Lit. Battistelli." A/B 1963. Repr: Kh 341 top. **17MN**
Variant: same in tinted rect. 8⅝ x 11⅜ **1**

GRASSI, Giovanni S 12CQ(?), 15PA, 16PA, 17CQPA, 18CQ see 271

GRISI, Carlotta (1819-1899) Ve 32-33, 34-35; F 33A, 34C; Na 34-36, 38-39; S 38A; R 47C see also 434, 453

*119 Full to L, facing front, body inclined to R, R foot pointe tendue croisée front, R hand behind waist, L arm up. Carlotta Grisi / Carnevale 1847. (no artists) A/B 2003. Repr: Kh 339. **MN**

120 (with her sister Ernesta) Two busts: Carlotta (on R) to front, facing slight R, eyes strongly R. Ferronière. Each: 7¼ in tinted rect. 8½ x 16¾. A/B 2010; 2011. **M**

GUERRA, Antonio (1806-1846) Na 22-23, 24-25, 29-30, 32-33, 34-35, 40-49; S 28PE, 29CQ; T 35 see also 350, 447

121 Bust to R, facing front. 4¼. (no artists). **M**

GUSMAN, Rosina Na 37; S 40PA, 41PA, 42PA; T 41-42; R 43A; Ve 45-46; Ferrara 47P; Trieste

*122 Full to R, facing front, attitude croisée back on L pointes. R arm up, hand amplified out, L arm chest height to R. 9½ in double rect. 12 x 9½. "Focosi"–Milano, Lit. Brison e Corbetta. A/B 2058. **MN**

123 Same pose, 4⅜. MUSIC COVER. Otto Quadriglie / Ridotte per Piano-Forte / Tratti dai Ballabili eseguiti dall / Sig.a Rosina Gusman / Nell I.e.R. Teatro degl'Immobili, in Via della / Pergola / da Carlo Ferranti / Firenze Presso Francesco Miniati, e figlio Da Badia. **1**

124 Full to R, facing front over L shoulder, 5th position on pointes, both arms to R, R up. 13¼. (her name, no other titling) (no artists) **NS**

125 Full to L, facing front, 4th position croisée on full pointes, hands crossed at bosom, flowers hanging from waist. 10⅞ in tinted rect. 12¾ x 8⅝. Rosina Gusman / In Ferrara la Primavera 1847. Ferr.,Litografia Zannoli. A/B 2057. **MS**

126 (with Auguste Lefebvre) Intricate frame surrounding a sonnet: "O archietto di detti atteggiamonti…". Pas de deux above: 3⅜. He:L; she:R. Their names on tambourines below. 13¼ x 10. C.Kunz e F.Bassi dis.– Lit. Linassi e C. Trieste. **S**

HEBERLE, Teresa S 25CP, 26CQA, 27CQPE, 28PE, 31CQA, 32CQ; T 25; Na 29-31 see also 405

127 Half to slight R, facing front, hair in curls under crown of braids. 5¼. Teresa Heberle / (quatrain:) "Le molli grazie del volante piede.…". D. Bossi dis. in Vienna–Per N. Bettoni-C. Cattaneo inc. A/B 2115. Repr: F/A II, 191. **1HMN**
Variant: same, but her name spelled "Eberle" **MN**

128 Bust to R rear, facing partly forward over L shoulder, double row of pearls in front of hair, swirling veil frames head. 4½. (Name) / Boucheron dis.–Locatelli inc. A/B 2116. **MN**

HENRY, Louis (or Luigi) (1784-1839) S 08CQ, 17CQ, 27CQ; Na 08-11, 12-13, 14-15, 18-21, 22-24, 27-28 (chor subsequently); Ve 27-28; M(Carcano) 31C see also 282, 299, 325

129 Nine busts including F. Galli, G. Donizetti, N. Molinari, G. Frezzolini, Giuditta Pasta, F. Romani, L. Henry, G. B. Rubini, V. Bellini. Omaggio al merito, in occasione della rappresentazioni date nel Carnevale dell' anno 1830-31 nel Teatro Carcano in Milano. Demarchi dis. dal vero– Rados figlio inc.–Milano presso Epimaco e Pasquale Artaria. A/B 347, 1329, 1654, 1743, 2123, 2923, 3295, 3937. **MS**

HENRY, Marie S 27CQ see 326

HORSCHELT, Barbara S 31CQ see 360

HULLIN, Jean-Baptiste m. Elise VAQUE-MOULIN S 21CQ, 22P; Ve 22-23, 25-27

130 (companion to 243) Bust to slight R, facing front, black cloak draped over shoulder. 2¾. G. B. Hullin / Ballerino. Aliprandi inc. A/B 2149. **M**

HUS, Pietro Na

131 Bust to slight L, facing up, high collar, looped tie. 3⅞ in circle 4⅜. Pietro Hus / Professore della regia scuola gen.le di balli / (quatrain:) "Tu chi il saper…" / Gli allievi tutti della sud.ta scuola / D.D.D. A/B 2155. Repr: F/A II, 179. **4MN**

KENEBEL, Virginia

132 Bust, directly to front, blond finger curls on both sides of forehead. 3⅛. Virginia Kenebel / Prima Ballerina di grazia. F. Spanoli dis.– A. Marchi inc. A/B 2219. (A Bolognese print). **MNS**

KING, Giovannina T 40-41; S 41CQPA, 42P, 43P, 47A; Mantua 43C; R 44A see also 439

133 (reverse of 439) Full to R, facing front, third arabesque sautée on R, double-layered skirt with two roses. 9½. All'Esimia Danzatrice / Giovannina King / Il Carnevale del 1842-3 nel Teatro Sociale di Mantova. R. Focosi lit.–Milano, Lit. Brison e Corbetta. **S**

*134 Full to slight L, facing front, arabesque sautée on L, L hand behind waist, R arm low and rounded. 11¾. Giovannina King / Prima Ballerina assoluta nel Teatro Valle in Roma l'Autunno 1844. V. Battistelli dis.–

Lit. Battistelli. A/B 2223. Repr: Kh 341 bottom. **4MN**

KUNZLER, P. Na 71; Ve 75

135 Full to R, facing front over L shoulder, seated, hands crossed in front of waist on a cushion. 10¾. (no titling). Lit. Rossetti—"F. Bignami." **N**

LAURATI S 63A, 65A; T 68-69   see 467

LEFEBVRE, Auguste Ve 29-30; S 32CQA, 33CQ, 34CQ, 40CQ; Trieste see also 126

136 Half to front, facing R, hair on chest above collar of costume. 7¾. Augusto Lefebvre / Primo Ballerino della grande Accademia Reale di Parigi / e primo Ballerino Francese nel grande Teatro dalla Fenice in Venezia / nel Carnevale 1830. Dalla primiata Litogr. Deyé. A/B 2340. Repr: Kh 71; F/A II, 183. **MN**

LEPRI, Giovanni Na; Genoa 52-56; R 54C; S 57CQ, 58A, 62CQ

137 Half to front, R hand under L elbow on chair back. 7½. Facs. sign. L. DeCrescenzo dip.–Lit. Wenzel. A/B 2377. **MS**

138 Almost half to slight R, facing front, small black bow tie. 6½. Facs. sign. / D.C.DDD / Carnevale 1854. Roma, Lit. Battistelli. A/B 2376. **M**

MAGLIETTI (or MAGLIETTA), Luigi and Teresa (née OLIVIERI q.v.) S 25P(he), 31CQ(both), 36CQ; Ve 31-32; Mantua 37; R 38C

139 (he on left) Each: full. He: L pointe tendue croisée back, arms in high 5th. She: 5th position on pointes, L arm high, R arm across waist. Each: 9. All'egregio merito / dei / Coniugi Maglietti / Primi ballerini danzanti / nel nobil Teatro d'Apollo / in Roma nel Carnevale del 1838. Lit. Martelli. A/B 2480. Repr: Kh 341, 2nd from top; Carr 53, lower L; MHW 102, bottom L. **16HMNPS**
Variant: same in tinted rect. 9¾ x 8½ **M**

MARCHESE (or MARCHESI), Nicola S 28CQ; Na; Bologna 30; Ve 42P, 43P   see 88

MARMET, Melina Verona 50; Ve 50-51; R 51C; S 52CQ

140 Full to R, facing L, arabesque penchée on R pointes, standing on globe or crescent moon. 8¾. M.lle Melina Marmet / dansava nel Teatro Filarmonico in Verona / l'anno 1850. Franc. Bonaldi dis.–Verona, Lit. Guelmi. A/B 2683. **MN**

141 Full to front, facing front, R foot pointe tendue croisée front, L hand on hip, R over head. 11. Melina Marmet / prima Ballerina nel Teatro di Apollo / in Roma nel Carnevale 1851. Lit. Danesi. A/B 2684. Repr: Kh 341, center bottom. **1HMN**

MARRA, Puride S (pupil) 43ff; M (Canobbiana) 47C   see 239

MATTIS, Domenico S 25CQ; Na 37; F 37A; Ve 37-38, 44-45; Genoa 42   see 36, 464

MAYWOOD, Augusta (1825-1876) S 48CQ, 49CQ, 53A; Ve 49-51; Trieste 50, 51-52, 54-55; Padua 51E; Bologna 51A; Ravenna 52; Ferrara 52P; Ancona 53P, 56P; Genoa 53; T 55-56   see also 142

*142 Full to slight R, facing L, sauté off of R, L foot in front, L arm up holds cup, R down with a pitcher. 10¼ in rect. 11¾ x 8⅛. Ad / Augusta Maywood / nell'Estate / in Padova anno 1851. (no artists). **S**

143 Half to slight R, facing slight R, figured dress with button in center button earring. 6⅛. ad / Augusta Maywood / la Società della Barcaccia nuova / offriva / nell'Autunno del 1851. G. Calza dis. dal vero—Minardi lit.–Lit. Via Ponte di Ferro 1055. Hall 1; A/B 2790; MHW, AM, 4. Repr: MHW, AM IV. **14HMNS**
Variant A: same, without "la Società della Barcaccia" **4**
Variant B: same, in tinted rect. 7¾ x 6¼. Augusta Maywood in Ferrara la Primavera del 1852. (same artists) A/B 2791; MHW, AM 9 **4M**

*144 (almost the same head as 143, reversed) Three-quarters to slight L, facing almost front, lace edging down f... of cloak, pendant earring. 7¼. Facs. sign. Vinc.o Poiret dis.–Lit. C. Malovich q. Kunz Trieste. **5**

145 (same figure as 143, but in costume) Point of bodice at waist has decoration which is reversed at center of rounded neckline, half sleeves on upper arm. 7. Ad / Augusta Maywood / Ravenna plaudente / 1852. "Miardi lit."–Lit. Angiolini. A/B 2792; MHW, AM 10 (A Bolognese print). **MN**

146 (same figure as 143, but different dress) Forearms disappear into vignette. 6½ in tinted rect. 9⅛ x 6¾. Augusta Maywood / Imparegiabile Danzatrice / in Ancona nella Primavera del 53. Litog. Maggi. MHW, AM 6. Repr: ibid. frontis. **N**

147 (same figure as 143, but in costume- different from 145; probably as Paquita) Stringed peplum on hips, shawl held in front. 6½. Ad / Augusta Maywood / Gli Anconitani nella Primavera del 1853 / (huitain:) "Dunque son finti i subiti timori...." A. Bedetti dis.–Ancona, Lit. Pieroni. A/B 2793; MHW, AM 11. Repr: Kh 234; Migel 34. **34M**
Varant: same on stone with rounded corners 9⅛ x 7½ (no artists) **N**

148 Full to R, facing front, head inclined L, balanced on R pointes, L foot croisé front, R arm up holds cup, L arm behind waist. 13¼ in ornamental frame which makes oval of rect. 16½ x 12¼. Ad / Augusta Maywood / nella Primavera del 1856 / in Ancona / Atto I, nel Ballo Rita Gauthier. "A. Bedetti"–Ancona, Lit. F. Pieroni. A/B 2794; MHW, AM 7. Repr: ibid. VI. **134MS**

149 (apparently related to 148) Half. MHW, AM 8.

MAZZARELLI, Fanny S 43CQP; Ve 43-45; R 52C

150 Short bust to slight L, facing front. 16 in tinted rect. 20 x 16½. Facs. sign. "Andretta dis."–Lit. Kier, Venezia. (verso:) "Primo saggio a due lapis..." A/B 2801. **M**

151 Three-quarters to front, facing front, R elbow on balustrade, L hand unfinished on skirt. 10¼. Facs. sign. / Al Gran Teatro d'Apollo il Carnevale del 1852 / Roma. Battistelli dis. e lit.–L. Izzoli Valentini dip. A/B 2799. **1M**

152 Full to slight R, facing front, gown, bouquet down in R hand. 16½. M.lle Fanny Mazzarelli (Janetti F.co dis. e lit.–Lit. Doyen e C. Torino) A/B 2800. **M**

MEMMI, Ottavio R 55P

*153 (with Pia Cavalieri) Each: three-quarters to inside. She (on R) facing front, head inclined L. He (on L) facing her. Inside arms clasped up, outside hands on hips. He: 7 in double rect. 12⅛ x 8¼. Ottavio Memmi Pia Cavalieri / di Anni 11 / nella Compagnia Senese diretta dal Coreografo F. Marrocchesi / in Roma. Teatro Argentina la Primavera 1855 / gli Amatori D.D.D. Battistelli dis. lit. A/B 063; 2820 **MN**

MERANTE, Adélaïde T 43-45; S 47A, 56CQ; Na 48-50, 51-52, 53-55

154 Half to, facing front seated, L forearm on chair back, R hand in lap. 7½. Facs. sign. L. de Crescenzo–Lit. Wenzel. **M**

MERANTE, François (most often Francesco) S 13-14, 15PA, 16PA, 17CQ, 41CQEA, 42CQEA, 43CQPA, 44CQA, 47A, 56CQ; T 43-45; Na 48-50, 51-52, 53-55

155 Three-quarters to slight L, facing front, R hand in striped vest. 8. Facs. sign. L. de Crescenzo dip.–Litog. Wenzel. **14M**

MERSY (also MERSY-QUERIAU), Adélaïde Na 08-09, 12-15, 14-15, 19-20, 23-24; Ve 25-26; F 28; S 32A, 33CQ

*156 (with Jean Rousset) Full, balanced on his R hip, in arabesque to L, facing R up, R hand holds end of garland which passes over her R foot and ends in his L hand. He: 8¾; she: 9. Alli SS Adelaide Mersy / Giovanni Rousset / per la loro Beneficiata la sera del 19 Maggio 1828 / nell'I.e R. Teatro della Pergola in Firenze / Zeffiro e Flora / (4 quatrains). Firenze Lit. Salucci n. 536. A/B 2847, 2899. Repr: F/A II, 175; NYPL Dance Coll., portfolio no. IX. **6MNS**

MILLIER, Antonietta S13CPA, 14CQPEA, 15CQPA, 16CQP, 17CQ   see 275

MOCHI, Davide S 42P, 52CQ; Ve 45-46; R 47A

157 Long bust to slight R, facing front, mustache, double-breasted vest. 6⅞. D.o–V. Battistelli. A/B 2989. **1M**

158 (similar to 157; but long tie and tie pin) 7¼. Davide Mochi / al Teatro Argentina/Roma autunno 1847 / D.P.DDD (no artists) A/B 2827. **M**

MOLINARI, Nicola S 11PAff, most seasons until 35CQ; Ve 16, 17, 29-30, 31, 32; M (Carcano) 31C; Genoa 36   see also 129, 283, 300, 304, ..., ..., ..., ..., ..., ..., ...

159 Short bust to front, facing L. 2⅞ in circle 3. (two verses:) "E pietade e terrer...." F. Caporali inc. A/B 2918. **M**

160 (companion to 168) Short bust to front, eyes slightly up, plumed hat. 7. Nicola Molinari / nell'Ines di Castro / Venezia nel Carnevale 1830. C. Rinaldi dis. A/B 2919. **MS**

161 Half to front, facing R, long hair to bare shoulders; arms clasped across waist. 6⅜. Niccola Molinari / Nel Ballo Imelda e Bonifacio. (no artists). **N**

MONTI CARESANO, Paolina S 36CQ, 46A, 47CA, 48CQ, 49CQ; Ve 38 (Oct.), 41-42; R 44; Na 44-46

162 More than half to R, facing front, single row of white flowers along top of bodice. 8½. Paolina Monti Caresano / Prima Mimica assoluta Roma 1844 / DC DDD. "V. Battistelli dis.—Lit. Battistelli." A/B 2968. **1MN**

163 Half to slight L, facing front, eyes slightly up, long hair, R hand clasps L forearm. 9¼. Paolina Monti / (two verses:) "Sul front…." Janetti F. lit.— Com per.—Torino, Lit. Junck. A/B 2969. **M**

MONTICINI, Marietta S 32A, 33A, 38P, 39CQ, 50CQ; F; Parma 37 see also 427

164 Bust to L, facing almost front, ermine sleeves, fur edge on bodice, stars around head. Sic itur ad astra / Marietta Monticini / nel Ballo Sofia di Moscovia. Lit. Saluzzi. A/B 2970. Repr: Kh 72 bottom. (A Florentine print). **1M**

MURATORI-LASINA, Gaetana S 37CQ, 39A, 40CQPA, 41CQPA. 42CPA, 43CQPA   see 424

NICHLI, Carlo S 1791Q, 16PA, 17PA, 18CQPA, 21CQA   see 269, 310

NOBLET, Lise

165 (after a French portrait by Grevedon) Half to very slight L, facing front, bodice crossed over at waist, complicated hat of lace, flowers and ribbon. 12. M.la Noblet / dell'Accademia Reale di Musica. H. Grevedon dis. dal vero—G. Rados figlio inc. A/B 3093. **1M**

OGGIONI, Felicità S (pupil) 33; Ve 43P; F 44P

166 Full to front, facing L, bad first arabesque on R, L arm down. 5. Felicità Oggioni / Prima Ballerina all hop.e R. Teatro Leopoldo / nella Primavera del 1844 / Firenze. (no artists). **M**

OLIVIERI, (sometimes OLIVIERI-BERTINI), Teresa (b. 1804) m. Luigi MAGLIETTI S18A, 19A, 20CQ, 21CQA, 22CQ, 23PA, 24P, 31CQ; Ve 24-25, 26-27; 31-32; Mantua 37; R 38C   see 139, 290, 462

PALLERINI, Antonietta (1790-1870) T 10, 27, 33, (poss. 36), 37, 38; S 13PA, 15CQ, 17Aff (most seasons until 26A), 31A, 32CQ, 36CQ, 38A, 39CQP, 40PA; Ve 18-19, 29-30, 33-35   see also 253, 284, 301, 305, 311, 401, 403, 408, 417, 422

*167 Full to front, facing L, holding two children. 7. Ines di Castro / Atto terzo. Two sides of medal below. 1⅝. Left: Alunna / delle Grazie / nella Mimica / Inimitabile. Right: her profile le R. her name and 1830. Eug. Bosa f.—Venezia, della premiata Litgr. Deyé. A/B 3223. **MS**

168 (companion to 160) Half to R, facing L, eyes strongly L, hair over L shoulder. 7. Antonietta Pallerini / Nell'Ines di Castro / Venezia nel Carnevale 1830. Carlo Rinaldi dis. A/B 3224. **MS**

169 Smoking urn atop a column. Whole: 14½. Ad Antonietta Pallerini / (quatrain:) "Quel premio a le Vinegia…" / anno MDCCCXXXIV / azione mimica i Veneziani in Costantinopoli. Venezia, litografia Barozzi. A/B 3225. **MS**

170 (companion to 209) Half to front, eyes up, hands clasped in front of bosom. 8. Antonietta Pallerini / (two verses:) "Prima nell'Arte, al sol girar de-rai…" P. Ayres"—Lit. di M. Ajello e C. / Carnevale 1828. (A Torinese print). **MNP**

171 (reverse of 284) 4¼. (her name) Gius. Longhi dis.—A. Comte inc. per N. Bettoni. A/B 3227. **HMNS**
Variant: same, reversed. 2⅞. (her name) per N. Bettoni. A/B 3228 **M**

172 Bust to full R profile. 2½. (her name) (no artists) A/B 3229. **M**

PAUL, Antoine (1798-1871) S 24A; Na 24-25; Ve 27-28

173 Bust from clouds, facing front, 3 plumes from beret. 8⅛ (to bottom of clouds). Paul / (four verses:) "Tu di Tersicore…" / Carnevale 1828. "Prepiani dis.—Butteraz lit."—Instituto litografico di Giuseppe Deyé a Venezia. A/B 3317. Repr: Kh 94 bottom. **HMN**

174 (companion to 204) Bust to front, head inclined R, 3 plumes, one falling to L. 3½. Antonio Paul. A. Ramacci dis.—G. Bozza inc. A/B 3318. **M**

PEAN, Paolina Ve 29-30; S 32CQ

175 Half to slight R, facing front, eyes up to R, complicated curls, at least 8 loops of bows in hair. 10¼. Paolina Pean / Venezia nel Carnevale 1830. Carlo Rinaldi dis. **1P**
Variant: same in tinted rect. 11 x 9½. A/B 3326. **M**

PECCI-AMBROGIO, Marietta Ve 37-39; Na 50(Aug.)

176 More than half to slight L, facing front, R hand on hip. 7⅝. Marietta Pecci-Ambrogio / Prima Ballerina assoluta del Real Teatro / della Corte di Dresda / In Napoli, Agosto 1850. L. de Crescenzo dis.—"Wenzel". **MN**

PEGHIN, Augusta m. Egidio PRIORA Ve 24-25 (named Francesca); T 29; S 35A; Ancona 39P; Ferrara 42P

*177 (with Egidio Priora; she on his R) Three-quarters to slight R, facing front; both seated, her L elbow on bolster, his R hand on her R shoulder. He: 5. Egidio Priora ed Augusta Peghen / Conjugi / Primi Ballerini Serii / Nel Teatro della Muse la Primavera del 1839. "ABedetti" (from Ancona). **N**
Variant: same, but….Coniugi / Primi Ballerini Assoluti / in Ferrara / la Primavera del 1842. A/B 3336, 3576 **MS**

PENCO, Francesco S 40P, 41P, 55P; R 44A; Ve 46 (Apr.), 53-54; T (poss. 45), 48-49; M (Canobbiana) 56P, 61P

178 Almost half to front, facing front, thick black tie. 6½ in tinted rect. 8¼ x 7. Francesco Penco / Primo Ballerino assoluto / Nel Teatro Valle l'Autunno 1844. V. Battistelli dis.—Lit. Battistelli. A/B 3354. **MN**

179 Half to R, facing almost front, long black tie, white vest. 7½. (his name) Janetti dis. e Lit.-con permissione 1845—Torino, Lit. Doyen e C. A/B 3357. **M**

PERROT, Jules (1810-1892) S 38A, 45CQ, 47CQ, 48CQ; Na 38-39 see 452

PEZZOLI (also PEZZOLI-ROLANDI), Francesca T 22, 36; S 22P; Ve 23-24, 38C; M (Carcano) 31C; R 35C; Genoa 36   see also 107, 206

180 Bust to front, facing slight L, veil from hair over L shoulder. 7¾. Francesca Pezzoli / Prima Ballerina Mimica / nel Teatro di Apollo nel Carnevale del 1835. G. Parisi dis.—F. Leante lit. A/B 3415. **145MN**

PIGLIA, Chiara R 32C; Bergamo 36 (Mar.)

181 Half to R, facing front, high square comb in hair. 9½. Chiara Piglia / Prima Ballerina assoluta per la Mimica e per la Danza / nel Nobile Teatro di Apollo nel Carnevale dell'anno 1832 / (quatrain:) "O muovi a danza il pie…"P. Guglielmi dis.—Roma, lit. Battistelli. A/B 3464. **3HMNPS**
Variant: same in tinted rect. 10⅞ x 8⅛ **1M**

182 Full to L, facing front, in Spanish costume with castanets, on L, R foot croisée front, R hand up, L down in back. 9. Chiara Piglia / Prima Ballerina Assoluta / per la Mimica e per la Danza / nel Nobile Teatro di Apollo nel Carnevale 1832 / (sestet:) "Cosi sotto uman velo…." / DDD. "Gajassi"—Lit. Battistelli. A/B 3465. **MS**

*183 Full to front, facing L, bare feet, L hand up with bow, feathers in headdress and on skirt. Chiara Piglia / (same as for 182) / (tercet:) Amor, speme, timor…" Lit. Battistelli a Roma—Gajassi dis. DDD. **HP**

PITTERI, Giovannina Verona 57C; S 64CQ

*184 Full to slight L, head inclined L, attitude front on L pointes, L hand under chin, R hand under L elbow. 12¼. Giovannina Pitteri / Carnevale 1856-57 / Verona / (two quatrains:) "Cosi ti libri sull'aereo piede…." Penuti fece dal vero—Verona, Pr. Lit. Penuti. A/B 3480. **1MN**

PLUNKETT, Adeline (1824-1910) Ve 55-56, 57-58; R 60C

185 Three-quarters to R, facing front, seated, hands folded in lap. 8½. Adeline Plunkett / Prima Ballerina Assoluta nel Teatro di Apollo Carnevale 1859-60 / Roma / Gli Ammiratori D.D. / Lit. Corso 145. "Battistelli dis." A/B 3490. **14HMN**
Variant: same in tinted rect. 10½ x 8¼ **M**

POCHINI, Carolina (1836-1901) m. Pasquale BORRI R 52C; Na 53-54, 66-68; S 54CQ, 55P, 57CQ, 59CQ, 60CQ, 63CQ, 66CQ, 71A; T 61-62, 66-67, 69-70, 73-74; Ve 66

186 More than half to slight R, facing front, R forearm on railing behind her. 6¼. Carlotta Ranieri Pochini / Prima Ballerina assoluta nel gran Teatro di / Apollo Carnevale 1852. Battistelli dis. e lit. A/B 3496. Repr: Kh 347 top. **1234HMN**
Variant: same in tinted rect. 9 x 7½ **M**

*187 Full to slight R, facing L, in soubresault, L hand up with bunch of flowers, R holds up skirt. 14½. A / Carolina Pochini / le Masse Artistiche del Teatro alla Scala / con l'arte potente ammirano …la Primavera del 1855. Facs. sign. (Carlotta Pochini) "Bignoli"— Milano, Lit. Vassalli. A/B 3497. Repr: Carr 55. **5MN**

Variant: same in tinted rect. 15¾ x 12⅛ **M**

188 Full to R, facing L, wings, star on head, standing on two dolphins in front of a shell, cascade of waterfalls in rear. Artist's proof for a Milanese newspaper, Aug., 1867. "V. Bignami." A/B 3498. **M**
A/B 3498. **M**

*189 (similar to 188) 6¼ in tinted rect. with irreg. corners 8⅝ x 7½. MUSIC COVER Idea / Ballo fantastico di Pasquale Borri / Rimembranze della Carolina Pochini / Nel Ballo Idea dal coreografo Borri. Milano lit. e Strada. **1**

190 (in same role and costume) Full, to complete L, facing slight R, hands crossed at bosom. 9 in oval 11¾ x 9. Galleria Artistica della Frusta Teatrale (quatrain:) "Vaga siccome un fior, casta siccome…" / Carolina Pochini / Nel Ballo Idea dal coreografo Borri. Milano lit. a Ronchi. **6**

191 Full to full R, facing over L shoulder, floor length crinoline, L arm rounded down, in front of a mirror. 4 in tinted rect. 6¼ x 4¼. (no artists) A/B 3499. **M**

192 Full to front. Soubresault, bare feet, arms low holding garlands hanging from shoulder, long pigtails flying. 6½ in double rect. 8 x 5⅜. Tersicore / Pochini, "Cam" (for Camillo Marietti). From a series of caricatures of the Muses. Countess d'Agoult as Clio on verso. **1M**

POCHINI, Elvira Pisa 53 (Aug.)

193 Three-quarters to slight R, facing front, R hand on column, long sleeves. A / Elvira Pochini / nel 18 agosto 1853 Serata a suo Benefizio / in Pisa…. / (verse:) "Alla che più non…" (no artists; or illegible: F. Ingavi?). **1M**

194 Half to slight R, eyes to very slight L, R arm across waist under L elbow. 7. Elvira Pochini / (quatrain:) "L'arte non solo qui ritrar sapea…." (no artists) A/B 3500. Repr: F/A II, 233. **MS**

POLIN, Adele Ve 42-44; (poss. S 50CQ)

195 Full to front, facing L up, 5th position on pointes, L arm across waist, R arm up. 10¾. Adele Polin / prima danzatrice / nel gran Teatro la Fenice Carnevale 1843. Lodi dis.–Lit. Kier. **MS**

PORTA, Luigia Na 17-18, 19-24, 25-26, 27-28, 29-33, 34-36, 37-38, 39-40; T 34-35

*196 Full to front, facing front, on demi-pointe of R foot, knee bent, L leg slightly extended in front, both arms in long gloves hold scarf over head. 8¾. Luigia Porta / (tercet) "L'agil suo pie…." / (Gli ammiratori). Con permissione 1834 Lit Aiello e Doyen. A/B 3533. Repr: F/A II, 203. **1MN**

PRIORA EGIDIO m Augusta Peghin S 26PA, 27CQ, 34A, 35A, 47A, 55CQ; Ve 30-31; R 32C; Ancona 39P; Ferrara 42P see also **118, 177**

197 Bust to L, facing slightly L, tie untied and crossed on chest. 5⅝. Egidio Priora / Primo Ballerino Assoluto / nel Nobile Teatro di Apollo nel Carnevale del 1832 / Omaggio al merito / (sonnet) "Egidio è questi…." Almerini.–Roma Lit. Battistelli. A/B 3575. Repr: Carr 51. **1MN**

PRIORA, Olimpia (b 1836) R 50C, 62C; S 55CQ, 61A, 70CQ; Ve 56 (Nov.); T 60-61, 65-66

198 Full to very slight R, facing front, head inclined L, on R pointes, L leg croisé front almost waist height, arms low 5th. 11 in tinted rect. 12 x 9¾. Olimpia Priora / Prima Ballerina Assoluta nel Teatro d'Apollo in Roma il Carnevale 1850. (no artists) A/B 3577. Repr: Kh 349 top. **M**

199 Three-quarters to R, facing front, seated, L forefinger against jaw. 7¼. Olimpia Priora / Esimia Prima Ballerina Assoluta / nel Teatro di Apollo in Roma / il Carnevale 1861 in 1862. Battistelli, Corso 145. A/B 3578. **1HMN**

QUAGLIA, Gaetana S 17 (pupil); 21CQ, 22CQ, 23A, 24CQPA, 25CQP, 26P see 291

RAMACCINI, Annunziata see BLASIS, Annunziata

RAMACINI, Antonio S 23P, 26CQP (all seasons to 31A), 31A, 34CQ, 36A, 37CQ, 41CQ; Ve 26-27, 32-33, 34-38; T 32, 39; M (Canobbiana) 33P see 340, 349, 411, 413, 420, 465

RAVAGLIA, Rosina Ve 41-42; Ancona 47P; R 47A; S 52CQ; Na 53-54; Fermo 58A

200 Full to R, facing front, third arabesque on R pointes, wings. 8. Rosina Ravaglia / Gli Anconitani la Primavera del 1847 / (quatrain:) "O mova il piede…." "F. Maggi"–Ancona, Lit. Dorica. A/B 3638. **M**

201 Half to L, facing front, tight bun at middle of back of neck. 6¼. Rosina Ravaglia / Esimia Danzatrice / che / nell'Autunno 1847 al teatro di Argentina in Roma / Colsi onori corrispondenti alle sue vertù. (no artists) A/B 3637. **1MN**

RAVINÀ, Ester S 16P, 21A, 24CQA, 25CQP, 45CQ; Ferrara 44P see also 210

202 Full to front, facing front, head inclined L, R hand on bosom, L arm up, R foot pointe tendue in 2nd; house behind to L. 14. Ester Ravina / (sestet). Massini dis.–Lit. Tary. **N**

REBAUDENGO, Clara S 22CQ, 24A, 25CQP, 26CQ, 34A; Reggio 26; Ve 28-29, 30-31 see also 294

203 Half to L, facing front, crown of braids, ruff. 9¼. "Reisener dis."–Milano Litog. Vassalli. **1S**

RINALDI, Lucia S 16CQ, 20P, 21CQ; Ve 27-28 see also 289

204 (companion to 174) Half to front, facing slight R, double strand of pearls, flower on L side of hair. 3½. (her name) A. Ramacci dis.–G. Bozza inc. A/B 3697. **M**

ROLLA, Teresa T 50-52; Genoa 56E; Ve 56-57; S 65CQ(?)

205 Almost three-quarters to front, facing front, R hand on hip, L forefinger to chin. 9¼. Teresa Rolla / Prima Ballerina Assoluta al Teatro Doria / l'estate del 1856, Genova. Genova, lit. Armanino. **H**

RONZANI, Domenico (1804-1868) Ve 25-26, 33-34; T 27, 28, 29, 31, 37, 38; M (Canobbiana) 30P, 31P; S 31A, 32CQ, 34A, 36A, 38PA, 39CQP, 40P, 45CQ, 49CQ; R 35C; Ferrara 44P see also 415, 416, 428

*206 (with Francesca Pezzoli) Full to front, facing each other; he threatening her with a knife in his upraised R hand. He: 7; she: 5¾. Domenico Ronzani e Francesca Pezzoli / Primi Ballerini Mimici nel Teatro di Apollo in Roma nel Carnevale del 1833. G. Parisi dis–F, Leante lit. A/B 3771. Repr: Kh 335; Carr 53. **MN**

207 Full to front, facing slight L, dagger from sheath which hangs from belt lying on floor, L arm up, R hand clenched down. 8½. (quatrain:) "Terribile così Ronzan parea/ …. E il freddo d'*Ezzellin* scegno fingea /…." Ant. Manuelli dis. e lit.–Roma Lit. Battistelli. A/B 3774. Repr: MHW, AM II. **1HM**
Variant: same in tinted rect. 10 x 7½ **M**

208 Full to slight R, facing R up, R arm to side, shield on L arm. 10¼. Ronzani. Lit. Matraire. A/B 3775. (A Torinese print). **M**

209 (companion to 170) Half to front, facing R, L hand on sword, R hand at chest. 10 in tinted rect. 11¾ x 8¾. (his name) / (couplet:) "Se le forti passion col gesto…" "Ayres pict."–Lit. di M. Ajello e C. A/B 3776. **M**

210 (with Ester Ravina) (He on L) Two busts to front, facing in toward each other, Islamic costumes. He: 6¼, in double rect. 10¼ x 15¼. Domenico Ronzani Ester Ravina / Primi Mimi Assoluti / in Ferrara la Primavera del 1844, anno primo della Fiera d'assegna. M. Domenichini dis.–Ferrara Lit. Zannoli. A/B 3773. **M**

ROSATI, Carolina see GALLETTI, Carolina

ROSATI, Francesco m Carolina GALLETTI Na 32, 34-35; Ve 36-37, 38-39, 40-42; S 39PA, 40CQ

211 (companion to 223) Long bust to R, facing front, one end of large black bow tie over L lapel. 5. Francesco Rosati / Primo Danzatore / al Gran Teatro la Fenice Carnevale 1838-39. Eug. Nap. Pianta dis.–Venezia, Lit.Kier. A/B 3804. **134HMSVe (Cor.)**

ROSSI, Adelaide R 57C

212 Three-quarters to slight R, facing front, open turban around coronet of braids, L hand holds eyeglasses along R forearm. 11¼. Adelaide Rossi / Prima Mima Assoluta al Teatro di Apollo / in Roma / Carnevale 1856-57. Danesi lit. A/B 3811. **1M**
Variant: the same in tinted rect. 12¼ x 8⅞ **M**

ROSSI, Giacomo see 107

ROTA, Giuseppe (1822-1865) Ve 49-50, 56-57; S 53Aff; R 55A see also 457

213 Three-quarters to R, facing front, seated, R hand in L side of coat, cane in L hand. 12½. Alcuni Ammiratori Frequentanti / Il Teatro Argentina Di Roma Nella / Stagione Autunnale Del 1855 / In Segno Di Stima / E Del Suo Gran Merito / Demano / Al Coreografo / Giuseppe Rota. De

Worsan dis.—Roma, Lit. Danesi. A/B 3893. **1HMN**
Variant: same in tinted rect. 13⅞ x 9⅜ **M**

214 (same as 213 but half length) "Vanzo dis." Milan lit. Corbetta. From newspaper *Un Soldo*, Dom.28 Maggio N.63. **S**

215 Half to slight L, facing front, seated, L arm over chair back. 7. A / Giuseppe Rota / nel Carnevale e Quadragesima 1854-55. Lit.Draghi (A Venetian print). **MS**

216 Bust to front, facing front. Giuseppe Rota morto a Torino 23 Maggio (1865). Bignami dis.—Vajani inc. A/B 3894. **M**

217 Bust to slight L, facing R, bulky black coat. 9 in rect. with rounded corners 10 x 7¾. "Bignami dis."—Milano Litog. e Fotog Manzoni—Illustraz.e Artistica del Giornale le Muse—G. R. **S**

218 Bust to slight R, facing front, scraggly mustache and beard. 6½. Wreath underneath with names of various ballets including *Bianchi e Neri.... Monte Cristo, Cleopatra.* Giuseppe Rota / (Vedi in Cenno biografico nella coplettina). "Ferrere." **S**

ROUSSET, Jean (or Giovanni) S 24A, 25CQP, 38P; F 28 (May); T28 see 156

ROZIER (often ROUZIER), Jean (or Giovanni) S 25CQ, 26CQ, 27CQPE, 31CQA; T 25; Ve 28-29

219 Bust to slight R, facing slightly L, eyes front, L hand in cloak. 6½. J. Rozier. Lit. Ricordi Milano—Pietro Fontana dis. A/B 2907. **M**

220 Bust to slight L, facing front, white collar of shirt over fur collar. 3. G.o F.o Rozier. A.Ramacci dis.—Antonio Nani inc. A/B 3908. **M**

SAINT-LEON, Arthur (1821-1870) T 41-44, 45-46; S 42A; R 43A, 45C; Parma 44 (Jan.); F 44 (Feb.), 45 (Nov.); Bologna 44 (Nov.); Ve 45, 48C

221 Half to slight R, facing slight R, double-breasted coat buttoned "woman's side." 7¼. Arthur Saint-Léon / Roma l'Autunno 1843. V. Battistelli del.—Battistelli Lit. A/B 3961. **15HMNR**

*222 Long bust to L, facing L, black vest with wide vertical stripes. 5. Arthur Saint Léon "Roma S.t Léon, 1845" A/B 3962. **1M**

SAINT-ROMAIN (also MEES SAINT-ROMAIN), Angelica S 37CQ, 38A, 39CQ; Ve 39C; Na 40-43   see also 425

223 (companion to 211) Half to slight L, facing front, head inclined to R, pearls high on neck. 4⅞. Angelica St-Romain / Prima Danzatrice / Al Gran Teatro la Fenice Carnevale 1838-39. Eug.Napol.Pianta dis.— Venezia, Lit.Kier A/B 3965. **1MNPSVe (Cor.)**

SALMOIRAGHI, Angela S (pupil) 63ff

224 Full to R, facing front, dress with long train, R fingers on column, L hand at waist; vegetation. 8. "V.Bignami" Proof before letters from a newspaper. A/B 3980. **MS**

SAMENGO, Paolo m.Amalia BRUGNOLI S 21A, 26P, 29PA, 30CQ; Na 26-27, 30-31   see 302, 451

SANTALICANTE (also PRISCO-SANTALICANTE), Raffaela m.Gaetano PRISCO Na 35-36, 37-39, 40-41; S 46CQ, 57CQ, 59A, 60CQA; Ve 46, 46-47; R 48C

225 Half to L, facing front, falling plume along R side of head. 8¼.Raffaela Santalicante / Prima Mima Assoluta / nel Ballo Renato d'Arles / Il Carnevale del 1848 in Roma / D. Camera D.D.D. (no artists) A/B 4031. Repr: F/A II, 215. **M**

SAPPINI, Antonietta Genoa 60 P; R 61P

226 Full to front, facing front, 5th position on pointes, fingers clasped, palms down; landscape with flaming urn and bust. 13½. Antoniotta Sappini / Prima Ballerina Assoluta al Teatro Andrea Doria / la Primavera del 1860 / Gli Ammiratori D.D.D. / (quatrain.) "Sei di un angelo...." Biaggio Torielli dis. e lit. dal vero—Genova, Lit.Armanino. **M**

227 Long bust to R, facing front, locket on thin chain, pendant earring L. 5¼. Antonietta Sappini / Prima Ballerina Assoluta di Rango Francese Roma / Nel Teatro di Apollo, Primavera / 1861. dis.Battistelli, Corso 145 A/B 4044. **1MS**

SCANNAGATTI, Carolina Novara 36; Ve 38   see also 107

228 (same costume as 107) Bust to L, facing front over R shoulder. Arms across waist. 7½. (her name) "A.C." A/B 4071. **M**

SCOTTI, Rosina Genoa 54P; S 55CQ; Ve 55-56

*229 Full to slight R, facing front, eyes up L, arabesque on R pointes, R hand to chin, L arm to side; foliage. 9½ in tinted rect. 12½ x 10½. A Rosina Scotti / La Primavera 1854 al Teatro Carlo Felice / A Genova. Torino 1854, Lit. F.lli Doyen e C. A/B 4126. **1MS**

SEGARELLI, Domenico (1820-1860) Ve 36-39, 45-46; T 42-43

230 Almost three-quarters to front, facing front, L hand gloved holds book across cloak. 10½ in rect. 12 x 10½. Domenico Segarelli / "Niun di te più bello e vago I nell'atto, nel gestir poter vestire I di *Kardinuto* eroe la strana immago. Janetti F.dis.—Galcaro lit.—Torino, con per.—lit. Junck. A/B 4134. **M**

SEVESI, Serafina S 16P, 17A   see 270

SOLDATI, Giuditta S 13CPA, 15P, 16CQP, 18CQ   see 262

TAGLIONI-PERAUD, Adélaïde m.Salvatore TAGLIONI Na 14-15, 17-20, 22-23, 24-25, 27-28; S 20P, 24A, 25CQ, 27PEA, 28CQ; T 31, 32   see 285

TAGLIONI, Luisina (1823-1893) (daughter of Salvatore and Adélaïde) m. Alexandre FUCHS Na 39-40 ff, 54-55, 57-58

*231 (with Eugenio Durand) Full to L, facing L, arabesque on L pointes; supported by Durand, leaning to L. each wears "?" (?) from the decoration of their costumes. She: 6¾; he: 5, in rect. with rounded corners 9 x 11. Autunno / Gruppo eseguito dalla Signora Luisina Taglioni ed il Signor Eugenio Durand nell' Opera Batilde di Turenna, nel Real Teatro S.Carlo / (two huitains) / L.E.Bardara. "De Lorenzo"—Filippo Del Buono dis. in. **H**

TAGLIONI, Marie (1804-1884) S 41P, 42P, 43CQ, 46CQ; Bologna 42A; R 46C   see also 444

232 Full to slight L, facing R, low arabesque sautée croisée on R, tambourine in L, R hand at L elbow to R. Maria Taglioni / nel ballo la Gitana / del coreografo Signor Filippo Taglioni padre della esimia artista. / (two verses:) "Chi vuol veder quanto..." "Focosi"—Milano,Lit.Gallina di Brison, A/B 4323. Repr: LM 64. **MNS**
Variant A: same in tinted rect. 20 x 10 **M**
Variant B: same but Bologna Litografia Bettini 1842 **NP**

233 Full to front, facing slight R, sauté on R, L up behind, R hand up, L down with castanets, deep décolleté, dancing on floor of large flagstones; panels of arabesque foliage on walls behind. M.lla Taglioni nel Ballo la Gitana. (no artists) **P**

*234 Almost three-quarters to L, facing front, R arm bent, hand on chest, L hand along R forearm, veil falling from wreath of white flowers. 7. M.Taglioni / ... tratta dal vero nell'autunno del 1842. A.Frulli dis.— Bologna, Lit. Zannoli. A/B 4324. **12HMNS**
Variant: same in tinted rect. 8⅛ x 7 **M**

235 (from London portrait by Edwin D. Smith—engr. by H. Robinson, dated Jan. 1, 1842) Three-quarters to front, facing front, seated, L elbow on cushion, R hand holds dog in lap. 8. Maria Taglioni / al Gran Teatro Apollo in Roma / il Carnevale 1846. "V. Roscioni litog." A/B 4328. Repr: Kh 107. **1MN**

TAGLIONI, Salvatore (1790-1868) Na 12-13, 19-20, 22-23, 30-31, 32-35, 37-43ff; S 24A, 25CQ, 27PEA, 28CQ   see also 286, 446

236 Bust to front, facing L, arms crossed. 3¾ in circle 4 diam. Salvatore Taglioni / al cui merito gli infrascritti suoi Aluni / della reale Scuola di perfezione di Ballo / D.no / Napoli, 16. Dicembre 1816. G. Morghen dis.e. inc. A/B 4349. **4MP**

*237 Almost three-quarters to front, facing front, R elbow on pillar with wreathed inscription: Nato / in Palermo / il 1791. L hand in lap holds roll with "Faust 1838." 8¼ in oval wreath of laurel leaves each one of which bears name and date of one of his 96 ballets. 14⅞ x 11¾. Facs. sign. L. de Crescenzo dis.—Litog. Wenzel. A/B 4351. Repr: F/A II, 187. **14MNS**

238 Bust, almost identical to 237, but coat buttoned to opposite side. From *Il Messaggiero della Moda / Giornale per la scelta Società* (Sem. 2.o— Num. 5), an unidentified periodical. It is not the Neapolitan *la Moda* of series M. **P**

*239 (with A. Ferrari and P. Marra) In circle, arms around each other's waist. Fifth position on pointes. 4 in floral rect. with rounded corners 13½ x 9½. Al Merito / di / Thierry Celestina, Ferrari Adelaide, Marra Puride / sulle scene dell' I.R. Teatro della Canobbiana nel Carnevale 1846-47 / (five verses:) "A Voi giovin Spere..." / "T.B.P." (no artists). **S**

TITUS, Catarino (also TITUS-DAUCHY) S 07A, 08QPE, 09P, 14PEA,

16CQP, 17CQP Ve 14, 15 see 275

TOGNINO Na 16 see 442

TORELLI, Antonietta S 13CPA, 22A; Ve 15, 16, 17, 18

240 Bust to slight R, facing front, hat with long plumes. 3⅛ in oval 3¾ x 3. (her name) / (two verses:) "Se Costei più l'Itale Scene onora...." (no artists) A/B 4456. **HMS**

TRABATTONI FINART, Anna S 28CQPE see also 326

241 Full to front, facing front, head inclined R, L hand behind back, R arm low. 7⅞ in rect. 9¾ x 7¼. (her name) Con permiso 1836–Torino, Lit. Ajello e Doyen. A/B 4484. **1MNS**

TREZZI, Gaetana S (pupil) 17, 20A, 21CQ, 22CQP; T 23 see 292

TRIGAMBI, Pietro S 15CQP, most seasons until 61CQ see 273, 320, 321, 347

TROIS GRACES (Taglioni, Elssler, Cerrito)

242 "There is, further, an Italian version that we have seen but did not note in detail...." Fr p. 201, under no. 110.

VALENZA, Carolina S (pupil) 18ff; 21CQA see 293

VAQUE-MOULIN, Elisa m. J. B. Hullin S 21CQ, 22P, 26P, 27A, 28A, 29CQ, 34CQ; Ve 21-23, 25-27, 35-36; Na 23-26, 27-28; T 28

243 (companion to 130) Bust to L, facing front, scarf around neck crossed through a ring at cleavage. 2½. E. Vague-Moulin. Aliprandi inc. A/B 4549. Repr: F/A II, 199. **M**

244 Half to R, facing front, complicated coiffure with two plumes and swaths of cloth, two necklaces. 6¼. Vague-Moulin Elisa. (no artists) A/B 4550. **1MS**

VESTRIS, Armand (1786-1825) S 04CQP, 05PE, 06CQP; Na 17-19, 22-23 see 443

VESTRIS, Auguste (1760-1840) see 449

VESTRIS, Bernardo (NOTE: the print catalogued A/B 4653 is listed under Gaetano Baldassare VESTRIS, a dancer, but is actually Bernardo, a composer. The print is described here to avoid confusion, but without number)
Half to front, facing front, seated, L arm over chair back, L hand holds folded music sheet down; R hand, below line of vignette, a cane (or baton). Facs. sign. "Focosi"–Milano Litog. Vassalli. 9½ in ornamented frame of a mask, weapons, tambourine, etc. 14 x 11½. **1M**

VIALE, Rosina R 71 (June); S 81CQ

245 A folded sheet. p. 1: A / Rosina Viale / egregia artista / in occasione della sua beneficiata / Roma, Giugno, 1871. p. 2: a sonnet. p. 3: Bust to front, facing L, earring with letter "R". 7½ in oval 10½ x 8½. "L. Machetti." A/B 4661. **M**

VIGANO, Ginevra Parma 43P; F 44E

246 Half to front, facing front, hat with bow on L, three plumes on R. 6½. (her name) / nel passo a solo il Sauting-Boll. Rivara Franc.o dis. i per comm.e di Calestani Gir.o–Vigotti Lit.a in Parma. A/B 4681. **M**

247 Half to slight L, facing front, band across forehead, earrings. 7¼ in tinted rect. 8¼ x 6¾. (her name) / Esimia Danzatrice / Al Ducal Teatro di Parma, nella primavera del 1843 / nel Ballo il Giaffar. Stamp.t alla Lit.a Vigotti e Comp.a. **M**

248 Full to R, facing front, on L pointes atop a wreath, R leg waist high, in 4th position front, R arm up, L across body to R. (her name) / Prima Ballerina assoluta nell I.e.R. Teatro / degli Intrepidi l'Estate del 1844 / in Firenze. D. Gaglier dis. **S**

VIGANO, Salvatore (1769-1821) see also 287, 303, 436, 437

249 More than half to R profile, facing R, R hand in opening of long buttoned vest. 5⅞ in oval 7 x 5½. Sepia. (no artists). **N**

250 Bust (1 inch high) atop a complicated column with bas-relief of kneeling woman with lyre, flames. Salvatore Vigano Neapolitano / Artifici scenico.... **S**

251 Bust to slight R, facing front. 2⅝. Above: A scene with at least 50 people at his burial. Two men lower a coffin into the ground. 13¼ x 18⅛. Tumulazione dell'Insigne coreografo Salvatore Viganò, O maggio piu unanimo.... **S**

252 Bust to L, facing front, two white collars. 4 in oval 4⅝ x 3⅝, the whole in rect. 6⅞ x 5. (his name) F. Caporali dis.–per Bettoni–A. Altini inc. A/B 4685. Repr: Kh 78. **1HMNS**
Variant A: same without rect. frame **M**
Variant B: same but A. Locatelli dis. **NS**

253 Bust to slight L, facing slight R, rect. locket on chest. 8½. (his name) / ritratto da un busto in marmo di Lorenzo Bartolini / dedicato alla celebre attrice Mimica / Antonietta Pallerini / ...Magni dis.–Milan, Lit. P. Bertotti. A/B 4687. Repr: F/A II, 207. **M**

254 (similar to 252) Half to slight R, facing front. 4 in oval 4⅝ x 3¾. (his name) / Coreografo insigne. G. Scotto in. A/B 4688. **MNS**

VIGANO, Virginia

255 Half to slight R, facing front, cross on black ribbon around neck, puffed sleeves. 10½. (her name) Gaet. Cornienti dis. **S**

VISCARDI, Giovanna S (pupil) 18-23 see 295

WALPOT (or VALPOT), Ferdinando Ve 53-54; Na 56-57, 58-61; M (Canobbiana) 55A; S 61A

***256** Full to slight R, facing R. 6 in tinted rect. 6⅝ x 4⅜. The whole in rect. 10¼ x 7. Ferdinando Walpot / all'I. R. Teatro alla Canobbiana / l'autunno 1855. litgo. Vassalli, Milano. A/B 4729. **MS**

ZACCARIA, Luigia Na 50-52; F 53E; Ancona 54P

***257** (with Ettore Barracani) She: kneeling in arabesque on R, facing L up. He: behind her, arms in high 5th. She: 6⅞; he: (to edge of her skirt which hides his feet) 4½. Primi Ballerini di rango francese / Luigia Zaccaria, Ettore Barracani / Nell I.e R. Teatro Nuovo, L'Estate de 1853. Lit. della Flora Firenze. **N**

258 Three-quarters to slight R, facing front, head inclined slight L, R hand on hip, L arm up. 7¼ in tinted rect. with rounded corners 8⅞ x 7. A / Luigia Zaccaria / nella Primavera dell'anno 1854 / gli Anconitani plaudenti / (sestet:) "Nei voli sei fantastica...." "F Maggi"–Litog. Maggi, Ancona. A/B 4765. **IIMP**

ZUCCHI, Virginia (b.c. 1857) T 67-68, 84-85; R 73A; S 74A, 76CQ, 83CQ; Na 79-81.

259 Half to front, facing front, arms crossed, locket at neck. 4½ in double oval 6⅛ x 4¾. Virginia Zucchi / Artista di Ballo / Roma Autunno 1873. Litog....H. LeLieure–Fotografia Danesi. **S**

260 Bust to front, facing front. From a newspaper. A/B 4799. **M**

261 Bust to front, facing slight R, braided frogs on front, flowing hair. 6⅛ in multiple rect. 9½ x 7½. "Pin"–Milano, lit. D. Bellazzi. **S**

PART 2

THE MILAN SERIES

SERIES A

Fasti del Regio Teatro alla Scala di Milano. Ballo Guidone Selvaggio ossia le Guerriere d'Alessandra. Fascicolo II (Milano, Per Sonzogno e Compagni, 1816). The 14 plates are given in Roman numerals. Performers are not named on the plates, but rather in the index to the volume. (They are given here in parentheses following the title on the individual plate.) Each plate bears the names: Pistrucci dis. ed inc.–Coloriti da Batelli e Fanf.i (or Fanfani. Whole book: **1S**

262 I. Regina delle Amazzoni (Giuditta Soldati).

263 II. Amazone.

264 III. Altra Amazzone.

265 IV. Altra Amazzone.

266 V. Amazzone vestita ad uso di Baccante.

267 VI. Una delle vedove degli uccisi compagni di Guidone.

268 VII. Una delle dieci mogli di Guidone.

269 VIII. Guidone Selvaggio (Carlo Nichli).

270 IX. Marfisa (Serafina Sevesa).

271 X. Grifone il bianco (Giuseppe Bocci) Grifone il negro (Giovanni Grassi).

272 XI. Uno dei 9 compagni di Guidone uccisi da Marfisa.

273 XII. Astolfo (Pietro Trigambi) Sansonetto (Filippo Ciotti).

274 XIII. Il Padrone della nave, che ha condotti i Paladini (Carlo Bianciardi).

*275 "Fuori dell'Azione". XIV. Primi ballerini (Caterino Titus Antonietta Millier).

SERIES B

Raccolta di 96 retratti di musicisti ed artisti di teatro pubblicata a Milano da Gio. Ricordi 1821. A volume with 96 plates in alphabetical series. The engravers of the group were Luigi Rados (1773-1840), who did the plates of the dancers, Antonio Conte (c. 1780-c. 1837), and Giovanni Antonio Sasso (fl. 1800-25). All those portrayed are presented bust length, c. 2⅛ in rect. 2½ x 2¼ with a text beneath. Only the first line of that text is cited (in quotation marks). Whole series: **MS**
Variant: The identical plates were republished, four to a page, as *Galleria Teatrale composta di XXIV Tavole in Rame contenente quattro ritratti per cadauna tavola de'più rinomati Maestri di Cappella, Cantanti, Attori, Coreografi, Danzatori, Professori di Musica, Pittori, ec.* (Milano Presso Giovanni Ricordi, MDCCCXXII). Whole series: **1**
This reprinting explains the occasional occurence of a "pair" of portraits. The list below gives the page number in the 1821 set, with the plate number in the 1822 series in parentheses.

276 p. 18 (T. XI, upper L) Maria Conti. "Vivacissima dotata d'agilità e di for—…" A/B 1049. Repr: Kh 76. **NS**

277 p. 19 (T. XVI, upper L) Giovanni Coralli (in same clothes and pose as 70) "Educato nell'ottima scuola francese otten—…." A/B 1064. Repr: Carr 44. **5NS**

278 p. 20 (T. XI, upper R) Teresa Coralli (in same clothes and pose as 71) "Tutt'anima tutta brio, capa—…" A/B 1067. Repr: Kh 73. **S**

279 p. 22 (T. XVI, upper R) Luigi Costa "Deve il sig. Costa annoverarsi fra il primi…" A/B 1102. Repr: Carr 44.

280 p. 28 (T. XI, lower L) (Antoinette Dupain) Antonietta Dupen / "Molto brio, molto espressione…" A/B 1378. **NS**

281 p. 38 (T. XXIII, upper L) Gaetano Gioja "Questo rinomato Coreografo ha lasciata molta…" A/B 1860. Repr: Carr 44. **1NS**

282 p. 42 (T. XVI, lower R) Luigi Henry "Agile danzatore ed intelligente compo—…" A/B 2122. Repr: Carr 44. **1NS**

283 p. 52 (T. XVI, lower L) Nicola Molinari "Il nome di Molinari suona famoso fra i dan—…". A/B 2917. Repr: Carr 44. **N**

284 p. 53 (T. XI, lower R) Antonietta Pallerini "Superiore ad ogni elogio, ad ogni confronto…" A/B 3222 (see 170). **NS**

285 p. 68 (22, lower L) Taglioni Peraud / "Fra la più leggiadre e gentili danzatri-…" A/B 4307. **4NPS**

286 p. 84 (22, lower R) Salvatore Taglioni "Agilissimo vivace e professore nell'arte…" A/B 4350. Repr: Carr 44. **5NS**

287 p. 92 (T. XXIII, lower R) Salvatore Viganò "Il nome di Salvatore Viganò in cima a tut—…" A/B 4682; Hall 1. **H**

SERIES C

La / Tersicore / Milanese / Anno I (Milano, presso P.e G. Vallardi, Cas. Marghe.ta, 1821). (Not 1824, as stated in A/B.) Short busts, each one a hand colored engraving, of eight female dancers in costume placed opposite dedicatory verses to them and their appearances in the ballets as noted below. Book: **NVe(Mar.)**

288 (frontis.) Adelaide Grassi (and poem, in *Timur Kan*) A/B 1964. **M**

289 (opp. p. 15) Lucia Rinaldi (and poem, in *la Pianella d'Argento*) A/B 3696. **M**

290 (opp. p. 19) Teresa Olivieri Bertini (and poem, in *Alessandro nell'Indie*)

291 (opp. p. 21) Gaetana Quaglia (and poem, in Ballo *Cid* (the title of the work was *Cimene*) A/B 3593. **M**

292 (opp. p. 24) Gaetana Trezzi (and poem, in *il Ciabattino di Montpellier* (the title of the work was *il Calzolaio di Mompellieri*) A/B 4494. **M**

293 (opp. p. 25) Carolina Valenza (and poem, in *la Capricciosa*)

294 (opp. p. 27) Clara Rebaudengo (and poem, in *Mirra*) A/B 3643. **M**

295 (opp. p. 29) Giovanna Viscardi (and poem, in *Il Pellegrino*) A/B 4707. **M**

SERIES D

A large group of long busts of theatrical personalities from Milan, roughly five to ten years later than series B, designed by Gallo Gallina and lithographed by the same Ricordi firm responsible for series B. Those known are not in costume. The high numbers on several of these point to a very large series. Others appear without numbers, suggesting the possibility of a later reissue. One of those listed below is found in a tinted rectangle, possibly from still another variant group. Those known are presented alphabetically.

296 (No. 580) Samengo Brugnoli Amalia. To L rear, facing front over R shoulder, plaid dress. 5⅞. Gallo Gallina-Litog. Ricordi. A/B 712. **1MN**

297 (unnumbered) Marietta Conti. To L, facing front, hat with many plumes falling to L. "Gallina"–Lit. Ricordi. A/B 1051. **M**
Variant: same in tinted rect. 7 x 5½ **1**

298 (unnumbered) Gaetano Gioja. To slight L, facing front, high rolled coat collar. 4¼. G. Gallina dis.–Lit. Ricordi–Milano. A/B 1861. Repr: F/A II, 171. **MN**

299 (No. 585) Luigi Henri. To slight L, facing up, double breasted vest under two coat collars. 5. "G. Gallina"–Lit. Ricordi. **1S**

300 (unnumbered) Nicola Molinari. To front, facing L, eyes up, high collar. 5. "G. Gallina" A/B 2922. **MS**

301 (unnumbered) Antonietta Pallerini. To full R, facing L front, high ruff. 5½. (no artists). **MS**

302 (No. 581) Paolo Samengo. To full L, facing slight L; chair back behind him. 4¼. Gallo Gallina–Litog. Ricordi. A/B 4020. **1HM**

303 (unnumbered) Salvatore Viganò. To slight L, facing front, high coat collar. 4¼. G. Gallina dis.–Lit. Ricordi–Milano. A/B 1861. Repr: **1MNS**

SERIES E

Raccolta di Figurini / ad uso dei Teatri / Giusta il costum di tutti tempi / e di tutte le nazioni….(Pubbl. in Milano dall'incisione Stucchi). The foreword is dated Milano, 24 luglio 1822; although that may be the date of the beginning of the publishing, many of the plates appeared much later. The series probably was issued in small groups like the Martinet plates in Paris. The order below follows that of the binding in the Marciana copy. (The names of the performers who portrayed the various roles are given in parentheses. They do not appear on the plates.) Whole series: **SVe(Marc.)**

GROUP: Costume Francese:

304 (no. 4) Ballo Gabriella di Vergy / Fayel Conte Francese del Secolo XII (Molinari).

305 (no. 5) Gabriella di Vergy (A. Pallerini).

306-307 (nos. 6 and unnumbered, but obviously no. 7) Soldati Francesi / del secolo di Filippo Augusto.

308 (no. 8) Elodia nel Ballo il Solitario.

309 (no. 9) Templare.

GROUP: Costume Inglese:

310 (no. 1) Ballo Giovanna di Arco / Talbot generale Inglese (C. Nichli).

GROUP: Costume Egizi:

311 (no. 1) Ballo Cleopatra / Cleopatre (A. Pallerini).

312 (no. 2) Re Egiziano / de'tempi remoti.

313-314 (nos. 3 and 4) Soldato Egiziano.

315 (no. 5) Gran Sacerdoto (Belloni).

GROUP: Costume Giocosi:

316 (no. 2) Il Noce di Benevento / Nel Ballo dello stesso Nome (Strega Martinazza) (Maria Bocci)—a tree with people in it.

GROUP: Costume Greci:

317 (no. 6) Donzella Greca / del Secolo IX.

GROUP: Costume Mitologici:

318 (no. 1) Amore Zeffiro e Favonio.

319 (no. 3) Bacchante—a female dancer in Arab costume.

SERIES F

Unknown title. Binding of the group at the Marciana in Venice reads *Collezione di Figuri Teatrali*. This group includes some of the plates from Series E and others, given below but without catalogue numbers, which refer to dance but not to specific ballets. Because of the premier dates of the ballets included, it must have appeared between 1827 and 1831. Many of the plates list "Lit. Ricordi," a few "Gallina dis." A dual system of numbering makes for great confusion. The "Cost. Inglesi" and "Cost. Francese" with the upper numbers of the first group, relate them to series E. The others (with the exception of those from *Arminio*) still bear two numbers but without notice of "Costume" series. The dual numbers are listed in parentheses below, separated by a slash: the one in the upper corner first; the one that appears below the title of the ballet second. (Names of performers of the specific roles are added in parentheses from the information listed in Gatti's *History of la Scala*.)
Whole series: **Ve(Marc.)**

GROUP OF NATIONAL DANCES: (Nos. 2 and 3) Costume Italiano / Danzante (no. 6) Costume Europeo / Danzante (a man on three-quarter pointes) (no. 10) Costume Russo / Danzante (a man) (no. 16) Costume Italiano / Danzante (a man) (no. 25) Costume Italiano / Danzante (a woman). None of these can be specifically identified as belonging to any particular ballet.

GROUP: Nel Ballo l'Assedio di Calais:

320 (7/61) Eduardo III armato (P. Trigambi).
321 (8/62) Eduardo III in abbito reale.
322 (9/40) Isabella moglie di Eduardo III (*sic*—the Queen of Edward III was Philippa of Hainault; his mother was the infamous Isabelle of France) (Bencini).
323 (10/39) Paggi e Dame.
324 (11/64) Giovanni de Vienne (Casati).
325 (12/57) Eustachio de Saint Pierre / maire di Calais (L. Henry).
326 (13/36) Costanza moglie di Eustachio (Marie Henry) e Alessio su nipote (A. Trabattoni).
327 (14/65) Aurelio (N. Molinari).
328 (15/36) Eleonora (M. Conti).
329 (17/71) Paesani.
330 (18/38) Archibesieri e Archieri.
331 (19/57) Scozzesi / Per il Ballabile.
332 (20/60) Borghesi (male).
333 (21/63) Guardia e Banda Reale Inglesi.
334 (22/41) Borghesi (female).
  collections: 1 (322, 327, 328, 334); S (320, 322).

GROUP: Nell Ballo Arminio:

335 (x/33) Donzella Cherusca.
336 (x/41) Varo generale Romano.
337 (x/32) Giovane Cherusco.
338 (x/38) Un Bardo Cherusco.
339 (x/39) Sacerdote di Giove.
340 (x/37) Arminio principe Cherusco (Ramacini).
341 (x/46) Soldati Cheruschi.
342 (x/40) Soldati delle Legioni di Varo.
343 (270/42) Confidente di Varo.
344 (x/35) Madri Cherusche.
345 (x/36) Vecchj.
346 (x/34) Thusnelda e Balder suo figlio.
  collections: 1 (337, 338, 344, 345); S (337).

GROUP: Ballo Gli Spagnoli al Perù:

347 (95/544) Ataliba re di Quito (*sic*—for Cuzco) (P. Trigambi).
348 (96/545) Zulica moglie di Ataliba (M. Bocci).
349 (97/546) Rolla duce de'Peruviani (A. Ramacini).
350 (98/547) Alonso Spagnolo rifugiato in Quito (A. Guerra).
351 (99/548) Cora moglie di Alonzo (M. Conti) e Fernando di lei figlio (Laurina Bonalumi).
352 (100/549) Sacerdote e Vergini del Sole.
353 (101/550) Popolo Cacichi Guardie.
354 (102/551) Pizzaro supremo duce spagnolo (G. Bocci).
355 (103/552) Carlo Fratello di Pizzaro (Goldoni).
356 (104/553) Almagno (Casati).
357 (105/554) Davila (Bianciardi).
358 (106/555) Ufficiali e Soldati Spagnoli.
  collections: 1 (350, 354, 356, 357, 358); S (352, 358).

GROUP: Nel Ballo Emma Principessa del Nord:

359 (61/915) Il Duca Bredislaw (G. Bocci).
360 (62/916) Principessa Emma promessa sposa al Principe Ratibor (Barbara Horschelt).
361 (63/917) Principe Ratibor (Casati).
362 (64/918) Il Genio delle Montagne (Gagliani).
363 (65/919) Amore (DeVecchi).
364 (66/920) Principe Ratibor in abito di caccia.
365 (67/921) Genio delle Montagne trasformato in Cavaliere.
366 (68/922) Genio delle Montagne alla danza.
367 (69/923) Genio delle Montagne trasformato in Montanaro.
368 (70/924) Cavalieri al Torneo.
369 (71/934) Banda.
370 (71 and 72/925 and 926) Soldati Cacciatori.
371 (73/927) Genio del Fuoco.
372 (74/928) Araldo.
373 (75/929) Porta Insegne.
374 (76/930) Porta Bandiera.
375 (78/932) Genio delle Montagne vestato alla Greca.
376 (79/932½) Corpo di Ballo.
377 (80/931) Genii de'Metalli.
  collections: 1 (360, 361, 364, 365, 366, 367, 368, 369, 370, 371, 373, 376, 377); S (371, 376).

GROUP: Nel Ballo la Vedova nel giorno delle nozze:

378 (127/822) Ferdinando, Re di Castiglia.
379 (128/823) Isabella, regina di Castiglia.
380 (129/824) Eleonora Dama di Cordova.
381 (130/825) Lorenza Figlia di Eleonora.
382 (131/826) Don Pedro Ricco Signore di Cordova.
383 (132/827) Mendoza Giovane Scudiero.
384 (133/828) Pietro Confidente di Mendozza.
385 (134/829) Laura Confidente di Lorenza.
386 (135/830) Dame.
*387 (136/831) Damigelle.
388 (137/832) Guerrieri Spagnoli.
389 (138/833) Paggi.
390 (139/834) Contadine.

391 (140/835) Contadini.
392 (141/836) Capo dei Musulmani.
393-394 (142 and 143/837 and 838) Soldati Musulmani.
395 (144/839) Guerriero Spagnolo.
396 (145/840) Trombettieri.
397 (146/841) Borghesi di Cordova.
398 (147/842) Carceriere.
399 (148/843) Donne di Cordova.
400 (149/844) Ragazze e Ragazze di Cordova.
collections: 1 (381, 383, 384, 386, 387, 389, 390, 391, 398, 399, 400); N (400); S (385).

SERIES G

I.R. Teatro alla Scala / Almanaco / per l'anno 1822 (Milano, Presso di Fratelli Ubicini). The first of a series of yearly almanachs that continued until at least 1838. The plates feature full length colored engravings of singers and dancers about 3" high in rect. 3⅛ x 2⅛. The name of the performer appears at the top; the role below, and the title of the work in parentheses below that. The run of the series is not complete even at la Scala, although enough of it exists there to divide it by years.

YEAR 1822:   S

401 (opp. p. 63) Pallerini / Giovanna d'Arco / (nel ballo Giovanna d'Arco).
402 (opp. p. 81) Giuseppe Bocci / Priammo / (Nel Ballo la Morte d'Ettore).

YEAR 1826:   S

403 (opp. p. 27) Pallerini / Nefte Regina d'Egitto / (Nel Ballo Sesostri).
404 (opp. p. 45) Molinari / Fernando / (Nel Ballo Bianca di Messina).
*405 (opp. p. 81) Héberlé / 1.a Ballarina / (Nel Ballo la Statua di Venere).   1
406 (opp. p. 97) Bocci / Creonte, Re di Tebe / (Nel Ballo Antigone).

YEAR 1827:   S

407 (opp. p. 51) Molinari / Paolo Malatesta / (Nel Ballo Francesca da Rimini).
408 (opp. p. 87) Pallerini / Dircea / (nel ballo di tal nome).

YEAR 1828:   S

409 (opp. p. 61) Conti / Regina delle Amazzoni / (nel ballo le Amazzoni).

YEAR 1829:   S

410 (opp. p. 45) Conti / Neala / (nel ballo il Paria).   M
411 (opp. p. 65) Ramacini / Arminio / (nell ballo i Cheruschi).   M
YEAR 1830: (unlocated, but the following print must come from it).
412 Conti / Cora / (nel ballo I Spagnoli nel Perù) A/B 1050.   M

YEAR 1831:   S

413 (opp. p. 33) Ramacini / (nel ballo) / Baiazet A/B 3618.   M
414 (opp. p. 53) Conti (in travesty) / (nel balletto) / festa da ballo.
415 (opp. p. 77) Ronzani / (nel ballo) / l'Orfano di Ginevra A/B 3769. M
YEAR 1832: (unlocated, but the following print must come from it).
416 Ronzani / Gusmano / (Nel Ballo il Rinegato Portoghese) A/B 3770. M

YEAR 1833:   S

*417 (opp. p. 7) A. Pallerini N. Molinari / Ines Don Pietro / Nel Ballo Ines di Castro. Demarchi—Lit. Bertotti.   1

YEAR 1834:   S

418 (opp. p. 15) Bocci / Colombo / (Nel Ballo il Colombo).
419 (opp. p. 45) M. Conti / Edwige / (Nel Ballo Guglielmo Tell).
420 (opp. p. 67) Ramacini / Romeo / (nel ballo Giulietta e Romeo).

YEAR 1835:   S

421 (opp. p. 80) Molinari / Eufemio / (Nel Ballo i Saraceni) A/B 2920. M
FROM UNKNOWN YEARS:

422 (prob. 1837) Pallerini / Bianca / (Nel Ballo Bianca di Castiglia) A/B 3226.   M
423 (prob. 1838) Molinari / Marco Visconti / (Nel Ballo Marco Visconti) A/B 2921.   M
424 (prob. 1838) Muratori / Elvira / (Nel Ballo I Minatori di Salerno).   S
425 (prob. 1838) St.-Romain / Costume Cracoviano / (Nel Ballo Romanoff).   S

SERIES H

The success of the Ubicini series caused the publication of rival ones. Here are grouped together two different almanachs. *Teatro Carcano / Carnevale del 1830-31 / Almanacco / per l'anno Bisestile 1832 / (Milano / per Gaspare Truffi e Comp / 1831).*   M

426 Molinari / nel Kao-Kang. 2¾.
Galleria Teatrale d'Italia / Almanacco per l'anno 1833 / (Milano, presso Carlo Canadelli. Contr. dell'Agnello No. 965).   MNS

427 (opp. p. 84) She: in feathered skirt and headdress, struggles against his hands grasping her wrists. 2. Monticini Catte / Pin...e trascina seco la misera Azena / Cristoforo Colombo. Repr: Cohen, p. 564.

SERIES I

Strenna Teatrale (later years add *Europea* to the title). Another series of yearly almanachs, which began in 1838 and which continued at least until 1847. We have not found a complete run. (N has 1838, 40, 43, 45, 46, 47) (M has 1838, 40, 41, 43).

428 (1st year 1838; opp. p. 163) Ronzani. Full to front, facing L, R arm up, L down. 4¼. A/B 3772.   MNS
429 (2nd year 1839) Fanny Cerrito. A reduced version of 47, very slightly shorter. 2¾. C. Sommariva dis.—Gaet.no Cornienti inc. A/B 884.   NS
430 (1839) Luigia Colombon. Half to front, facing L, seated in a Gothic chair. 4¼ (to top of chair). A/B 1028. Repr: Kh 340; F/A II, 221.   MS
431 (3rd year 1840) Carlo Blasis. A reissue of 16.   MN
432 (9th year 1846; opp. p. 105) Lucilla Grahn. (From a Danish original used for a French print published in *les Belles Femmes de Paris*, vol. I: Fr. 40) In *la Sylphide*. The wings are now over her L shoulder; there is a wreath in her hair which is different; clouds at bottom are more pronounced. 4. Cornienti inc. A/B 1946.   MN
*433 (1846; opp. p. 161) Amalia Ferraris. Full to front, facing front, in cabriole back with R, arms in high 5th, wreath in R. 4½. Cornienti inc.   MN
434 (10th year 1847; opp. p. 144) Carlotta Grisi. Half to front, facing up, seated, book in lap; garden with fountain behind. 3⅞ in rect. 4⅞ x 3⅞. (no artists).   MNS
435 (1847; opp. p. 179) Fanny Elssler. Half to front, facing L, seated, L hand with bouquet at L shoulder, R hand supports mandoline. 4½ in rect. 6 x 4. Chevalier lith.   N

SERIES J

Ritorni, Carlo, *Commentari della vita e delle opere coredrammatiche di Salvatore Viganò* (Milano, Guglielmini et Redaelli, 1838). Book: **IHMNS**

*436 (frontispiece) A marble bust, 1⅜, atop a column; 3 other columns in rear before a "Temple to Glory." (untitled) In rect. 6¾ x 3¾. Lit. Bertotti. A/B 4684.
437 (title page) Half to slight R, facing slight L, R forearm on table. 2⅞. (untitled) G. Bignami dis.—Lit. P. Bertotti. A/B 4683.

SERIES K

Figaro / giornale / di letteratura, Belli Arti, etc.... so reads the title of the Cerrito item listed below. The other three, somewhat later, bear individual numbers rather than dates from the newspaper.

438 (Sabbato, 21 marzo 1840 / Anno VIII—numero 24) (Fanny Cerrito) related to 47 and 429. Half to slight R, facing front, seated. 4. (Below: her biography.)   S
439 (No. 3) Galleria Artistico-Teatrale / Giovannina King. Reverse of 133. Focosi dis.—Somariva eseg. Milano, Lit. Brison e Corbetta—Milano, Tip. Guglielmini. Repr: LM 71.   N
440 (No. 5) Galleria Artistico-Teatrale / Annunziata Ramacini-Blasis. Half

to front, facing slight L, R hand holds roll of music on table, L hand with handkerchief across waist. 8. Milano–Tip. Guglielmini. **S**

441 (No. 9) the same but Carlo Blasis. Bust like 14 but 5¾. **S**

THE NAPLES SERIES

SERIES L

An unidentified series of small costume plates similar to the Martinet engravings of Paris (Fr. series A). The two numbers listed below are identical in size and format. The period of time between the two ballets represented suggests a much larger group.

442 (No. 3 in upper R) Tognino nel ballo del Sig.r Des chalumeaux / Real Teatro del Fuoco / (three dotted lines with no text) / Atto Scene. Full to R, facing R, dancing on L foot, R foot pointe tendue 4th front, elaborate 18th century court costume with brocaded coat, sword and muff. 4⅜ in double rect. 5⅞ x 3¾. (anagram:) MC(?)-1816. **12**

*443 (No. 8 in upper R) Armando Vestris nel ballo di Macbeth / da esso composto / Real Teatro di S. Carlo / Musica del Conte di Gallemberg Barbaja Impressario. Full to front, facing L profile, dancing on both demi-pointes, R knee bent, balanced on point of sword held down R, L hand clutching chest. 4¾ in double rect. 6 x 4. "LM". **N**

SERIES M

La MODA / Appendice al Poliorama Pittoresco. A supplement, issued every two weeks (later, every ten days) to the *Poliorama pittoresco / opera periodica / diretta ed illustrata dalle classi / della Società / Napoli / dalla Tipografica e litografica del Poliorama Pittoresco* (Filippo Cirelli direttore prop.) The parent magazine appeared weekly from August, 1836. La Moda began on June 1, 1839 and continued to Oct. 10, 1844, under the director-owners G. Falvelli and D. de Giurnay. Whole series: **Na(Libr.)**

Year I (June 1, 1839-May 31, 1840).

444 (No. 1–June 1) Maria Taglioni (and biography pp. 1-3). Half to front, facing slight R (from a Paris portrait in a faint plaid dress). 5¼ (no artists). **N**

445 (No. 7–July 30) Amalia Brugnoli-Samengo (and biography pp. 25-27). Half to slight L, facing slight L, double chain necklace with pendant of 3 pearls. 5½ in tinted rect. 5⅞ x 5⅛. (no artists). **1**

446 (No. 18–Nov. 20) Salvatore Taglioni (and biography pp. 69-71). Bust to front, facing front in robe with double collars. 4½ in tinted rect. 5⅞ x 5 (no artists). **1**

447 (No. 30–Mar. 20, 1840) Antonio Guerra (and biography pp. 117-119). Bust to R, facing front, wide collar and lapels opened wide across chest. 5⅝ in tinted rect. 5¾ x 5. (no artists). **1H**

448 (No. 33–Apr. 20, 1840) Gaetano Gioja (and biography pp. 129-132). Bust (no artists).

Year II (nothing).

Year III (June 1, 1841-May 31, 1842).

449 (No. 12–Sept. 20, 1841) (Auguste) Vestris (and biography pp. 45-47). Bust to front, facing up L, long curls and Roman headband. 4¾ in tinted rect. 5⅝ x 4⅞. G. Riccio lit. (from a full-length French study in the *Galérie Théâtrale*, No. 46, Fr 508). **1**

Year IV (June 1, 1842-Aug. 10, 1843).

450 (No. 14–Oct. 15, 1842) Fanny Elssler (and biography pp. 53-56 signed "Psiche") (in *le Diable boiteux*) Three-quarters to front, facing R, R arm up, L arm down. G. Riccio lit. Full page. (from a full-length French study in the *Galérie des Artistes dramatiques*, No. 5, Fr 540).

451 (No. 15–Oct. 25, 1842) Paolo Samengo (and biography pp. 57-60). Bust to L, facing front, very high collar with points against jaw. 3½ in tinted rect. 5½ x 5. G. Riccio lit. **HS**

452 (No. 16–Nov. 5, 1842) (Jules) Perrot (and biography pp. 61-63) (as Zingaro). Almost three-quarters to front, facing R, L hand ? at hip. 4½ in tinted rect. 5¾ x 4⅞. G. Riccio lit. (from a full-length French study in the *Galérie des Artistes dramatiques*, No. 12, Fr 539). **1S**

Year V (Aug. 1, 1843-Aug. 10, 1844).

453 (No. 13–Sept. 20, 1843) Carlotta Grisi (and biography pp. 14-16). Full to R, facing front, arabesque sauté on R, flowers falling from hands held in front. G. Riccio lit. (the reverse of a full-length French study in the *Galérie des Artistes dramatiques*, No. 63, Fr 543). **4**

454 (No. 23–Apr. 5, 1844) Fanny Cerrito (and biography pp. 90-92). Full to L, facing front, floating under ballooning cloak (similar to 55). 6⅝ in tinted rect. 6 x 5⅛. G. Riccio lit. **1**

Six weeks after the publication of Cerrito, No. 454, the parent magazine, the *Poliorama pittoresco*, reissued the portrait:

455 (*Pol. pitt.*, No. 41–May 18, 1844, p. 321) (different biography pp. 322-323). It is a variant only in the quality of the paper and the printing. G. Riccio lit. A/B 889. **1M**

THE TURIN SERIES

SERIES N

Galleria Teatrale delle Scintille. A series of prints published in *Le Scintille Gazzetta della Sera*.

456 (No. 21) Natalia Fitz-James. Almost full to slight R, facing front, L hand across holds veil around body. "Follis"–Lit. F.lli Chapusot. A/B 1605. **M**

457 (No. ?) Giuseppe Rota. Half to slight R, facing front, R forearm on table, long chain around neck to below waist. 6⅞. "Dugnia" (?)–Lit. Giustina e Saltaselia (?). Between four scenes from his ballets, clockwise: Un Fallo (upper L), Il Giocatore, Bianchi e Neri, Il Conte di Montecristo. **P**

SERIES O

Galleria Teatrale. A possible continuation of the previous series. Obviously from a newspaper, as there is text on the verso of each print. It is possible that 458 comes from still a different group.

458 (*Galleria Artistiva Teatrale*, Torino, 1856) Catterina Beretta. Three-quarters to L, facing front, seated, hands in lap, L elbow on table. 9¼. "C. Teja"–Lit.a F.lli Chapuzot. A/B 390. **M**

459 (same without "Artistiva", 1856) Amina Boschetti. Full to R, facing L, L foot pointe tendue in 2nd, R arm up, L arm across with castanets. 10½. "Daniele" A/B 605. Repr: E/S II, 866. **M**

*460 (same, 1857) Augusta Maywood / (sestet:) "L'aereo pie che il suol par che non tocchi...." Full to front, L foot pointe tendue 4th front, R hand behind waist, L hand holds skirt out. 10. "Daniele" A/B 2795; MHW, AM 12. **1M**

THE VENICE SERIES

SERIES P

Teatro / Della Fenice / Almanacco Galante / Dedicato alle Dame (Venezia–Presso Giuseppe Orlandelli Editore). Aliprandi inc. Book: **S**

461 (opp. p. 16) C. Blasis. Bust to slight R, facing front, tunic held on each shoulder by a boss. 3¾. A. Viviani dis.–F. Zuliani inc A/B 499. Repr: E/S II, 608. **MVe(Cor.)**

462 (opp. p. 21) T. Olivieri. Bust to R, facing front, cloak with boss on L shoulder, two bands across hair. 2⅝. F. Zuliani inc. A/B 3139. **MVe(Cor.)**

SERIES Q

Album / Per Ricordari l'apertura del Nobile Gran Teatro / Della Fenice (Venezia, 1827-38) on cover. Title page: *Dodici principali artisti / della Stagione / di carnavale e Quadragesima 1837-38* (Venezia, Imp. R. Pr. Litogr. Barozzi–A Magnaroni scr. e inc.) Each plate presents a bust of the artist within a complex, ornamented frame comprised of 4 antique masks, musical trophies in clusters, and, at top center, an eagle with wings displayed appearing above a flaming bowl. 11¾ x 9¼. Book: **7S**

463 (plate 9) Antonio Cortesi. Bust to R, facing front, velvet collar high in back. 4¼. Eug.o Nap.e Pianta dis.–Venezia I. R. pr. Lit. Barozzi. **1**

*464 (plate 10) Dom.co Mattis. Bust to right, facing front. 4. (same artists) A/B 2762. **1M**

465 (plate 11) Ant.o Ramacini. Bust to L, facing front, bushy mustache, short beard, coat with frogs and flat fur collar. 4¼. (same artists). **1M**

466 (plate 12) Amalia Brugnoli Samengo. More than half to front, facing front, veil hanging from hair falls to waist over R shoulder. 4⅞. (same artists). **NVe(Cor.)**

MISCELLANEOUS

467 Unnamed female dancer (probably Laurati) on stage. Full to R, facing back over R shoulder, R forefinger points to shipwreck in rear. 5¼. MUSIC COVER. La Tempesta / Ballo del Coreografo P. Borri / Musica del Maestro A. Baur....Torino, Giudici e Strada. **1**

EDWIN BINNEY 3RD

Since the publication of *Dance Perspectives* 47, the author has read a paper titled "Giselle, Apothéose de Théophile Gautier" at a symposium commemorating the centennial of the death of the great French ballet librettist and critic. The symposium took place at the University of New Mexico, Albuquerque, in October, 1972. Mr. Binney has also been performing the mime roles of Madge in *La Sylphide* and Drosselmeyer in *The Nutcracker* with the San Diego Ballet.